That The Two May Become One

*36 Wedding Sermons Sharing
the Good News of God's Love*

John R. Nagle

CSS Publishing Company, Inc.
Lima, Ohio

That The Two May Become One

FIRST EDITION
Copyright © 2020
by CSS Publishing Co., Inc.

Library of Congress Cataloging-in-Publication Data:

Names: Nagle, John R., 1943- author.
Title: That the two may become one : the good news of God's love shared with the happy couple / John R. Nagle, B.A., M. Div., D. Min.
Other titles: Sermons. Selections
Description: First edition. | Lima, Ohio : CSS Publishing Company, Inc., [2020] | Summary: "Here is a creative way of sharing God's Word and practical advice in the life ahead for couples on their wedding day, and an anniversary-day review for those already married. Amid formal wear, beautiful flowers, guest lists and toasts, it's easy to lose focus of what the wedding day could be all about. These scripture-based words of encouragement and promise, often given in a refreshing manner, can be a life-long reminder for the bride and groom"-- Provided by publisher.
Identifiers: LCCN 2020000066 | ISBN 9780788029707 (paperback) | ISBN 9780788029714 (ebook)
Subjects: LCSH: Wedding sermons. | Lutheran Church--Sermons.
Classification: LCC BV4278 .N34 2020 | DDC 252/.1--dc23
LC record available at https://lccn.loc.gov/2020000066

For more information about CSS Publishing Company resources, visit our website at www.csspub.com, email us at csr@csspub.com, or call (800) 241-4056.

e-book:
ISBN-13: 978-0-7880-2971-4
ISBN-10: 0-7880-2971-1

ISBN-13: 978-0-7880-2970-7
ISBN-10: 0-7880-2970-3   DIGITALLY PRINTED

Praise for
That The Two May Become One

The Reverend Doctor John Nagle served as pastor of Christ the King Lutheran Church in Cary, North Carolina, (until retirement) leading a small mission congregation to one of the largest Lutheran congregations in the southeastern United States. During that time, Dr. Nagle delivered many wedding sermons and these are some of his best!

These winsome sermons begin with an illustration to connect those gathered with the couple and the world around them and move quickly to scripture and proclamation of God's word. A distinction is made between this joy-filled wedding day and the days of marriage which follow. While the wedding is glorious, there will be times in the marriage that are not glorious and these sermons provide counsel and suggestions on how they can prepare and respond when it is "better" or "worse"! The love of Christ the king is shared, often using scripture chosen by the couple, to explain how Christ should be a part of the growing/changing relationship of marriage.

These short and concise sermons, wordsmithed by Dr. Nagle, would serve as good counsel for any couple preparing to spend their lives together. In fact, these sermons would be helpful to any couple in a serious relationship or long-time married. I appreciate these sermons of grace and wisdom written by a loving caring pastor who "tells it like it is"!

Leonard H. Bolick,
Former Bishop, NC Synod,
Evangelical Lutheran Church in America

With depth, warmth and humor, John Nagle's preaching touches our hearts, enlivens our relationships, and surprises us with powerful insights that strengthen our relationships of love with one another and with God. A book to be treasured, these sermons are fresh, lively, and filled with deep wisdom.

Anne-Marie Neuchterlein, M.D, Ph.D., Author

Couples' Bible study. Gift for newlyweds. Anniversary gift. Marriage counseling. This little book of wedding sermons is a delight, a revelation, and a must for numerous audiences. Whether considering marriage or in it for fifty years, an insightful compendium of biblically based advice.

Sandra R. Cline,
Call Process Coordinator, NC Synod,
Evangelical Lutheran Church in America

The question asked is more important than the answer found at times. This is a core message of the Reverend Doctor John Nagle's preaching and teaching for as long as I have known him. In these brief homilies, he gets young couples embarking on the journey of marriage to look at life a bit differently than perhaps they had anticipated. The messages call us to take personal responsibility for the marriages we create. The best part, though, is that he gets all couples to stop and reflect on how they are living out their marriages. Just married or married 36 years as I am, these homilies will make you smile, think, and maybe live just a little differently.

Don Fernando Azevedo
Ph.D. Clinical Psychologist and Marital Therapist
Azevedo Family Psychology

Contents

Foreword

The question has often been put to me, "So, how many weddings have you done?" It's a well-intentioned query, asked by people who have seen me as the lead pastor at a number of marriage events. But there are so many other (and maybe better) questions that probably should be asked of someone who presided at worship services uniting two people in love. These are some of the questions: Did anything unusual ever happen? Yes, but none of it bears remembering, except by the people involved. Do you remember your first wedding, over forty years ago? Yes, as if it were yesterday. Did all of the couples manage to celebrate their fifth or fifteenth or silver wedding anniversaries? No, they did not. What do you think is the reason that marriages don't always last? Likely, the bride and groom didn't listen to the scripture lessons that were read or to the homily that was preached at their wedding. Not that paying close attention to those words would guarantee happiness and longevity, but it's a good start.

I've collected some of the sermons I preached during my years as advisor to new husbands and wives. And I've done so in the thought that brides and grooms just starting out on their life together may find them helpful, even as brides and grooms celebrating long years of marriage may find them reflective. A number of these homilies use the same scripture lesson, often the thirteenth chapter of the New Testament letter to the Corinthians or the third chapter of the letter to the Colossians. But even though the scripture readings are the same, the application of those verses is not. Then too, in reading through my collection of wedding sermons, I find that I have repeated some themes, not because I could think of nothing new to say, but because the theme seemed to match the man and woman in front of me.

In each sermon that follows, I have chosen not to identify the happy couple — at least because some of the people who first heard these words are now neither happy nor a couple. But the intention is the same. And these are holy words: that the two may become one.

John R. Nagle   February 14, 2020

What It Means To Be Tied Up

Ecclesiastes 4:9-12 – *Two are better than one, because they have a good reward for their toil. For if they fall, one will lift up the other; but woe to one who is alone and falls and does not have another to help. Again, if two lie together, they keep warm; but how can one keep warm alone? And though one might prevail against another, two will withstand one. A threefold cord is not quickly broken.*

From the very beginning, you told us what is important. It was stated right there on the invitation. You could have emphasized the festivities of the day, or the lavishness of the day or the expense of the day, but you didn't. Instead of telling us what to expect at your wedding, you told us what to expect in your marriage. And this is what that scripture from Ecclesiastes says: A cord of three strands is not quickly torn apart. Yes, and that's where your strength will come — that one and one have come together to make two. And that two have come together to make one. But the presence of the third is what gives your marriage strength. It's Christ who makes the cord strongest. And I presume you think that a strong cord is something good.

There are dozens and dozens of uses for a cord that binds, some of them good and some of them bad. To be bound with someone you love is good. To be confined in a relationship you hate is bad. To be wrapped up in a task can be good. To be trapped doing something distasteful is bad. To be tied can be good, but to be tied up is not. So the question before you today is, In this whole matter of binding, to what do you want to be tied? To each other, of course, and to the Lord too. Tied to the past? Probably not. Tied to your families? Less than before. Tied to your employment and your hobbies and your friends? A bit. But there are priorities. We know you can't be tied deeply to everything, nor should you be. Scripture says, For this cause of marriage a man shall leave father and mother and cling to his wife. And the wife will cling to her husband. That sounds like an inconsistency. That there's an unbinding that leads to a binding. But that's the way it is with life. That some things begin and others end. That some things wrap and some come loose. That there's a time for everything, and that wisdom understands what and when that time is. And understands most of all what it is that makes our binding tolerable and wonderful and loving and eternal.

And is it not the example of Christ who pulls us tightly to himself? He binds us to himself with a pleasant cord, and nothing that strangles. It's a binding that will not let go, no matter how much we might work against it. It's a binding that offers strength and sustenance, something that endures through good and bad, something that gives without requiring in return. And that's what is primary in your marriage, isn't it? That you follow where he has led the way. That you choose to be with each other, bound up with Christ and his people, the church. Never alone, always accompanied. Which is another aspect of it, you see. On this day when you bind yourselves to each other, know that you are also tied with others around you who care about you, who pray for you, and who hope for your future. This is the Body of Christ, the people of God throughout history and around the world. Some of them have left you a good example. Some of them invite us to learn from their sadness. All of them rejoice in three cords that bring strength. The two of you, and Christ. Faith, hope, and love. The past, the present, the future. Creator, redeemer, sanctifier. And on it goes. Cords of three strands that bind us together. Cords that will not be broken.

That's what you wanted us to know. In the vows you have written, in the lessons you have chosen, in the worship order you have created, that's what you wanted us to know. And that's what we'll expect to see. That's what will sustain us and you in these days ahead. So may God, Father, Son, and Holy Spirit, keep you in his light and love now and forever. Amen.

And When You're Fifty Years Older

1 Corinthians 13 – *If I speak in the tongues of mortals and of angels, but do not have love, I am a noisy gong or a clanging cymbal. And if I have prophetic powers, and understand all mysteries and all knowledge, and if I have all faith, so as to remove mountains, but do not have love, I am nothing. If I give away all my possessions, and if I hand over my body so that I may boast, but do not have love, I gain nothing. Love is patient; love is kind; love is not envious or boastful or arrogant or rude. It does not insist on its own way; it is not irritable or resentful; it does not rejoice in wrongdoing, but rejoices in the truth. It bears all things, believes all things, hopes all things, endures all things. Love never ends. But as for prophecies, they will come to an end; as for tongues, they will cease; as for knowledge, it will come to an end. For we know only in part, and we prophesy only in part; but when the complete comes, the partial will come to an end. When I was a child, I spoke like a child, I thought like a child, I reasoned like a child; when I became an adult, I put an end to childish ways. For now we see in a mirror, dimly, but then we will see face to face. Now I know only in part; then I will know fully, even as I have been fully known. And now faith, hope, and love abide, these three; and the greatest of these is love.*

Lots of people are getting married today. The month of May is a popular time for brides and grooms. Virtually all of those couples will be able to celebrate their first-year anniversary next May. Most of them will make it five years. Only a relative few will celebrate their golden anniversary. I wonder what it will be like for the two of you on May 18, 2052. Interestingly enough, that date falls on a Saturday too.

I won't be there, and neither will your parents. Only a very few of the people here today will be present to celebrate with you. That shouldn't matter. A one-day party, even after fifty years, is less important than the celebration that lasted throughout the fifty years. If there were any celebrating, that is. Brides and grooms are obviously happy and excited on the day they get married. It's the next day or the next week or the next year that is the problem, for it happens that marriage gets ordinary. And ordinary is okay if it's special. Let me say that again. If the life you two lead is special, special every day, special every year, then the special becomes the ordinary, the usual, what you expect from each other and with each other. But to have that relationship, you need to work at it. And that's what we heard read in the scripture lessons today.

We heard that love is intended to be patient and kind. But it isn't always. Love isn't supposed to dwell on hurt, but we sometimes do. Love is intended to think of others before the self, but lots of us fall short with that. Husbands and wives are to live together in mutual love and respect, with a sacrifice that mirrors Christ's own. And on this first day, maybe all of that is so. Will it be that way on your fiftieth wedding anniversary? I can't say. The world then will be different. You will be different. Will your love stay the same? I hope not. Not that it gets less, but that it grows more. I don't make fun of you when I say that you don't know very much right now. You know enough, but I assure you that there's more. If you'll work to discover it, and share it, and celebrate it, you'll find there's more. The world will have changed, and you will have changed, and your love may have changed. But the love of God will remain the same. And modeling that unchangeable love can make all the difference for the two of you.

Will you mess up? Of course. Will it be serious? Probably. Will there be pains and anger and fears along the way? I suppose so. Will any of that make any difference? I don't know. It sort of depends on whether you want to reach your fiftieth wedding anniversary intact, with each other. If you make lists of hurts, if you try to be boss, if you snap at each other or fail to pay attention, if you spend time doing things that won't last, you won't make it. Your emphasis will be on the present, and not on the future.

The scripture lesson talked about the present and the future. It said that now we see dimly, incompletely, but that later on we will see fully. Actually, the reference there isn't to how you understand your fifty years together, but to how you understand God who cares so much about your marriage — who cares even more about the two of you than you care about each other. We don't understand that now, because we think there's nothing more wonderful than the two of you, nothing more special than the love you share. But we're wrong, for the love of God is stronger and greater and deeper and more long-lasting than anything you exhibit. And if you understand that, and if you depend on that, and if you share like that with each other, May 18, 2052, will be a good day

14

indeed. For on that day, you'll be over seventy years old. And people may think that you're wise. At least you'll be experienced. And what will you tell the people around you? The same things these people today will tell you?

That as children of God, you are loved by God who waits to strengthen your every day together. This day. Tomorrow, and that special Saturday in May, 2052.

If I Text Or I Tweet Or I Chat

1 Corinthians 13 – *If I speak in the tongues of mortals and of angels, but do not have love, I am a noisy gong or a clanging cymbal. And if I have prophetic powers, and understand all mysteries and all knowledge, and if I have all faith, so as to remove mountains, but do not have love, I am nothing. If I give away all my possessions, and if I hand over my body so that I may boast, but do not have love, I gain nothing. Love is patient; love is kind; love is not envious or boastful or arrogant or rude. It does not insist on its own way; it is not irritable or resentful; it does not rejoice in wrongdoing, but rejoices in the truth. It bears all things, believes all things, hopes all things, endures all things. Love never ends. But as for prophecies, they will come to an end; as for tongues, they will cease; as for knowledge, it will come to an end. For we know only in part, and we prophesy only in part; but when the complete comes, the partial will come to an end. When I was a child, I spoke like a child, I thought like a child, I reasoned like a child; when I became an adult, I put an end to childish ways. For now we see in a mirror, dimly, but then we will see face to face. Now I know only in part; then I will know fully, even as I have been fully known. And now faith, hope, and love abide, these three; and the greatest of these is love.*

When my father was in his mid-eighties, he lived in a retirement home. Wanting him to know that I was accessible at all times, I told him if he ever needed to talk to me to call me on a number that I handed him. I gave him my home phone and my office phone number. I also gave him my cell phone number. I felt secure and certain that we would always be in touch, even without telling him about my email address and my twitter account and my Facebook page. With all those resources, how could we not stay connected? But you know, even with all that, my father hardly ever called. Maybe it was his confusion; maybe the number of possibilities was overwhelming; maybe he just had nothing to say. Though I'm sure the two of you have something to say. Or you should. Consider the scripture lesson we heard read.

Saint Paul wrote, *If I speak in the tongues of men and of angels, if I call or I write, if I text or I tweet, if I chat or I skype, no matter how many ways there are to connect with each other, if it is done without love, it is nothing. Or worse than nothing, it is like a noisy gong or a clanging cymbal.* Not that there's anything wrong with talking to each other only on a cell phone, but that sometimes the connection isn't as great as the static and the call is sometimes dropped. And where is the love in that? Nor is there anything inherently wrong with only email, though I'm not sure it counts as conversation. And where is the love in that? Oh, there's Facebook — but isn't what I write more often about my own face than yours? And where is the love in that? And though I can see your face when we skype, I don't get to touch and hold you. Without that, where is the love? Though the point is not simply by what means we communicate, but what we express. Paul said, it's best about love. Love that is patient when there's no cell tower around. Love that is kind, even when an email should be erased. Love that does not boast on a blog or a homepage. A love that is shared even in spite of technology. Love that bears all things, believes all things, hopes all things, and endures all things. Love that never ends.

But you know about love that never ends, or so you tell us today. Here you pledge to each other an affection, a desire, a dream, a promise, a connection that you say will go on and on. And that's something good. Today, that's something easy. But know that it may not be as easy tomorrow, certainly will not be as easy in the years ahead. Even knowing what should be and how it could happen, well — you might end up like my father, who knew the numbers to call, but didn't always follow through. But you'll follow through, if you agree with St. Paul that love is something you give, more than you get. That love is something you feel, more than something you read about. That love is something you won't fully understand but should engage in anyway, and in every way. Always looking for <u>new</u> ways to love and to be loved in return. For, if I had offered these words to you a decade ago, I wouldn't have spoken about Facebook and skype. And in a decade yet to come, there may be other examples to use, unknown to us right now. The technology will change, but the love must not, if you hear and understand a basic example, and mirror it.

Which, you see, is the greatest gift you'll receive today. Nothing from your guests or your family or me, but the love that St. Paul knew about when he wrote about the love that should be yours. The love that comes to you from God. God who has loved you from the beginning and who vows to love you to the end. God who loves you when you are distant and who himself promises never to be distant. God who gives without expectation of return. Except that you should act as he does. Giving and forgiving, nurturing and supporting, offering back the compassion, kindness, humility, and patience first offered to you, and being accessible at all times. Asking God to be accessible to you. Being accessible to each other. That is what love is all about. That you give to each other what was first given to you. And that you use the gift. In all of the ways that you can, that you use the gift.

Whether you speak in the tongues of men or of angels, of theology or technology, this day and every day, let this be what you say to each other: As God has loved me, so I love you. So I love you.

Can You Overdose On Love?

John 15:9-17 – *As the Father has loved me, so I have loved you; abide in my love. If you keep my commandments, you will abide in my love, just as I have kept my Father's commandments and abide in his love. I have said these things to you so that my joy may be in you, and that your joy may be complete. This is my commandment, that you love one another as I have loved you. No one has greater love than this, to lay down one's life for one's friends. You are my friends if you do what I command you. I do not call you servants any longer, because the servant does not know what the master is doing; but I have called you friends, because I have made known to you everything that I have heard from my Father. You did not choose me but I chose you. And I appointed you to go and bear fruit, fruit that will last, so that the Father will give you whatever you ask him in my name. I am giving you these commands so that you may love one another.*

I went to a restaurant the other day and they were advertising something called Chocolate Extreme. It was made of chocolate fudge ice cream with chocolate chips with pieces of chocolate brownies inside. Now, I figure that all that chocolate would either make you happy or make you sick; it sort of depends on how you feel about chocolate. That makes it something like love. Are lots and lots of love something good or not, something that will make you happy or sick? It sort of depends on how you feel about love.

I'm not worried about today. I am not even worried about you. After all, you have chosen as a scripture lesson something that speaks of love. A scripture lesson some people think seems to overdose on love. Love one another because God has loved you and if you love one another, then people will see the love that God has for you and keep on loving each other as a model of your love and God's. That is quite a mouthful, even if it is something that sounds appropriate for this day. Though some people may think that all that talk about love sounds a bit extreme, something like a sickening too-sweet dessert.

Now, you may be surprised that anyone feels like that. But if you look at the statistics, apparently, lots of people get sick of love. There are people who figure that love is for themselves and not for anyone else. Some people figure that love is for now and not forever. There are people who figure that love has a long memory about things that are best forgotten. Other people figure that love should get old even as they themselves do. That's who gets sick of love. People who have failed to grasp the meaning of the scripture lesson you chose and people who don't understand the goodness of love that is extreme. But it's that extreme love we wish for the two of you today.

It is extreme love that gives without expecting to be loved back. It is extreme love that doesn't worry about whose turn it is. It is extreme love that is a gift and not an obligation. It is extreme love that mirrors Jesus' sacrifice and extreme love that for you should be ordinary. Not ordinary as in dull and uninteresting, but ordinary as in usual and normal and constant. Nor is that double-talk, to say that extreme love should be ordinary. It's not nonsense at all, because it's the way that God has already loved us. For in an extraordinary way God's love has become the norm and example for us and for you. Extreme love - our extreme love which models God's extreme love. That means that going out of your way actually is the way. Loving too much is never enough and that loving the other means loving yourself. In experiencing extreme love, your joy will be complete.

That's our gift to you, what we hope for you every day. In truth, there may be trials in your life and crises with your love. But that's just why we ask God to send you his extreme love, that you may know it, show it, share it, keep it, and delight in it the rest of your life together.

And Sometimes Things Break

1 Corinthians 13 – *If I speak in the tongues of mortals and of angels, but do not have love, I am a noisy gong or a clanging cymbal. And if I have prophetic powers, and understand all mysteries and all knowledge, and if I have all faith, so as to remove mountains, but do not have love, I am nothing. If I give away all my possessions, and if I hand over my body so that I may boast, but do not have love, I gain nothing. Love is patient; love is kind; love is not envious or boastful or arrogant or rude. It does not insist on its own way; it is not irritable or resentful; it does not rejoice in wrongdoing, but rejoices in the truth. It bears all things, believes all things, hopes all things, endures all things. Love never ends. But as for prophecies, they will come to an end; as for tongues, they will cease; as for knowledge, it will come to an end. For we know only in part, and we prophesy only in part; but when the complete comes, the partial will come to an end. When I was a child, I spoke like a child, I thought like a child, I reasoned like a child; when I became an adult, I put an end to childish ways. For now we see in a mirror, dimly, but then we will see face to face. Now I know only in part; then I will know fully, even as I have been fully known. And now faith, hope, and love abide, these three; and the greatest of these is love.*

Someone is going to give you a set of fine goblets as a wedding present. Please understand that the time will come when one or more of them will get chipped or broken. Someone will give you some cookware in a color that's in vogue right now. Please understand that in a few years that color will seem to clash with everything else you own. Someone is going to give you some bedding, towels, or some other linens. Please understand that at best they're going to fray, and at worst fall apart in your hands. And what will you do then? Well, you may put the stuff out for a yard sale. It's the American way.

Although that hasn't always been the American way. It used to be that if something were broken, we'd try to fix it. If something lost its usefulness, we'd turn it into something else. But that was before consumerism took over. Now, with scarcely a thought, we get rid of what once was good. And I'm speaking now, not of goblets or linens, but of marriage. The scripture lesson I just read says that love never ends — and that's a beautiful thought. Unfortunately, the truth of the matter is that for some people, love does end, and sometimes fairly quickly. We ask ourselves, *What happened? They seemed like such a nice couple.* But some relationships break and some aren't in style and some just seem to fray and fall apart. Love is banished to the emotional equivalent of a yard sale so fast it makes your head spin.

It is not bad that things fray or break. In this imperfect world, it's what happens. But what is sad is that people don't know how to fix things, or more often don't have the desire or energy to fix them. Did anyone ever hear of mending — or is it too much trouble to take? If it is too much trouble, for whom? The scripture says that love never ends — but you know, the reference there isn't to the two of you and the vows you make. The reference is to the on-going goodness of God who will claim you as his own even when the two of you seem unable to maintain the vows you make. That promise of God may be the best present you'll get today. Certainly, we have proof that it's lasting. Can you imagine what life would be like if God had been as consumer-oriented as we are? Can you imagine what life would be like if God decided not to mend the ways we break with him? Can you imagine God putting us out on the curb because of our failures? Lord, didn't you say we were your own? Isn't that the promise from our baptism? Yes it is, and over and over in scripture we read that God's love never ends. Why then should our modeling of his example ever end?

Oh, some brides and grooms, misunderstanding all this, say that the best way to keep things from breaking is never to use them — and that makes a kind of sense. There are lots of goblets that sit in cabinets, never touched. It's true that what is never touched never breaks. But that's not the story I'm telling. Does it really make sense never to use something just because you want to keep it unspoiled? Does it really make sense never to enjoy something because of a fear that the enjoyment may change later on? Don't be afraid of breaking something or letting it wear out. The problem is not that something will break but that you may forget to depend on God and his mending when something does break or fray or pass from style. His love never ends. We know that he loves you forever. Make sure that your love of him is that long-lasting too.

Don't worry that you'll not have enough. Love is patient and kind — or at least it should be, though sometimes it is not. Love is not envious, boastful, arrogant, or rude. But we all know that sometimes it is. The threat to your marriage is that you'll be tempted to get rid of what you have. Perhaps you wonder why I speak to you like this. Shouldn't my words be positive and uplifting on this most special of all days? Yes. And the goblets you'll get are all shiny and the cookware is still in its box. The linen has that nice new look and smell. It's easy to say nice things today and tomorrow too — maybe even next year.

But when everything else breaks, frays, and goes out of style, when nothing seems to make sense and you wonder what life is all about, when you shudder to think of commitment and wonder if eternity is a joke, when you're tempted to say that it's all over and there's nothing left, remember that God doesn't outfit yard sales with his children. For his love never ends.

If The Bride And Groom Go Shopping

Colossians 3:12-17 – *As God's chosen ones, holy and beloved, clothe yourselves with compassion, kindness, humility, meekness, and patience. Bear with one another and, if anyone has a complaint against another, forgive each other; just as the Lord has forgiven you, so you also must forgive. Above all, clothe yourselves with love, which binds everything together in perfect harmony. And let the peace of Christ rule in your hearts, to which indeed you were called in the one body. And be thankful. Let the word of Christ dwell in you richly; teach and admonish one another in all wisdom; and with gratitude in your hearts sing psalms, hymns, and spiritual songs to God. And whatever you do, in word or deed, do everything in the name of the Lord Jesus, giving thanks to God the Father through him.*

While all of us are spending our Saturday here, a lot of other people are spending their Saturday at the mall or specialty stores or beach shops, some of them in a frenzy, trying to decide what to wear this summer. They are deciding whether they should follow their own style or dress like everyone else; whether to buy something extreme or something more laid back. They are deciding to choose something trendy or lasting, or even something from last year. And that's important because most people have already figured it out — that what you wear and how you wear it says a lot about how you are.

One of the scripture lessons you chose says this: *clothe yourselves with compassion, kindness, humility, gentleness and patience.* And that's good advice, of course. As good and attractive as clothing that's pictured in the paper, hung on the rack, or fitted on a mannequin. Though people never buy what's in the paper or on the rack or the mannequin, unless and until they actually try it on. They try it on to see that it fits. Nor does the Bible say that you should intellectually approve of compassion, kindness, humility, gentleness and patience. It says that you're supposed to put it on, like clothing, because what you wear and how you wear it says a lot about how you are.

If you have compassion, you'll spend more effort on other people than you do on yourself. A lot of us think that sacrifice like that is something good, and that caring about and paying attention to those who are in need is true to the example that Jesus gave us. So is kindness. Kindness that is second-nature: not something that you have to think about, but a way of living that is the norm. Humility gives us more trouble, because it's not our usual first pick. In truth, we like ourselves so much that we want to protect our own selves from all harm and danger. Though in marriage, you have chosen each other, are each other, and can give to each other, not worrying about your own self. You are not sounding a trumpet about your humility, your kindness, or your compassion, but living gently with each other and the world around you. But you're getting married in a time that isn't gentle. The people with whom you interact may wonder why you wear something like tenderness. Be patient with them, and maybe they'll understand why you do what you do — that what you wear and how you wear it says a lot about who you are.

Understand that if you clothe yourself in compassion and kindness, humility, gentleness and patience, what's important for you, you may be wearing what others do not. Those qualities aren't necessarily trendy. Indeed, why would the scripture even mention them, except that most people don't understand them? People don't understand them and don't wear them; they think they look funny. But if you're willing to try something new that is really something old, to try something today that you know will last forever, to be models of those who have gone before you, then the stuff you wear in your life together may actually be hand-me-downs.

That is what your parents hope, now that they have gotten you this far in life: that hand-me-downs aren't as bad as you think, and they actually count for a great deal. They hope that what your families have taught you, those things that scripture mentioned, may serve you and others as well as it has served them. Not that the people around you have always been compassionate, kind, humble, gentle, and patient. In truth, they have not. Nor will you always be clothed in what scripture says is good. But in your marriage, at least think about it and what it says. Think about how you should appear before God, your friends, and society as a whole. For what you wear and how you wear it says a lot about who you are. It speaks of who you are and whose you are.

May you ever shop for what is good, what is fitting, and what is beautiful, always looking for compassion, kindness, humility, gentleness, and patience — whatever clothes you well. Today you're all dressed up. People love to get dressed up for a wedding. But our prayer for you is that you'll get just as dressed up for your marriage, for your life together, now and forever. For what you wear and how you wear it says a lot about who you are, and who loves you. So says the scripture. So say we all.

The Bridal Couple's Emergency Kit

Colossians 3:12-17 – *As God's chosen ones, holy and beloved, clothe yourselves with compassion, kindness, humility, meekness, and patience. Bear with one another and, if anyone has a complaint against another, forgive each other; just as the Lord has forgiven you, so you also must forgive. Above all, clothe yourselves with love, which binds everything together in perfect harmony. And let the peace of Christ rule in your hearts, to which indeed you were called in the one body. And be thankful. Let the word of Christ dwell in you richly; teach and admonish one another in all wisdom; and with gratitude in your hearts sing psalms, hymns, and spiritual songs to God. And whatever you do, in word or deed, do everything in the name of the Lord Jesus, giving thanks to God the Father through him.*

A wedding — how nice. A wedding at the beach — how nice. A wedding at the beach at the height of hurricane season. Whatever were you thinking! Not that there's anything absolutely wrong with choosing such a date. Both of you are people whose families have known the coast for a long time. You all know what can and cannot happen, what the risks are, and what it takes to have things go well. You also know how important it is to have plans in place, a kit prepared for that time when something goes wrong. You need a kit with the right tools in place, a kit that will address the basics, a kit with what will sustain you, a kit that is always at hand. You need a kit you get ready in good times for that moment when bad times come. So it's common sense — that if the existence of a helpful and sustaining kit is necessary for beach-time weather, it's even more necessary for a beach-time wedding. And for the life-long marriage that follows. It's something you've got to have.

For in truth, there will be times over the next fifty or more years when you will need to depend on that emergency preparedness kit. There will be a time when not everything the two of you face will be wonderful. Though it may seem that only an unkind person would spoil this wonderful day by telling you that not every day ahead will be this wonderful, it's something we all know. And you should know it too.

There will be times in your marriage when you don't see eye to eye. There will be times in your marriage when your energy is insufficient for whatever task is before you. There will be times in your marriage when something threatens your well-being. There will be times in your marriage when you fear being trapped or flooded or blown away, without anything at hand to offer comfort, hope, and sustenance. More than one marriage has foundered during some terrible storm because there was no thought given during the good days to what could save and make a difference during the bad days.

But the two of you must have thought about all that, because you chose for our hearing today a portion of scripture that tells you what should be included in your own emergency preparedness kit. Whether or not you chose that reading because someone else said it was good, whether or not you chose it because you heard it read at someone else's wedding, whether or not you chose it because you had to pick something, the fact is that if you pay attention to those words, you're well on your way to surviving the storms you'll face. Not avoiding the storms, but surviving the storms you'll face. You cannot avoid trouble, but if you pay attention to scripture, you can survive trouble.

You can survive trouble if you clothe yourselves with compassion, kindness, humility, meekness, and patience. That's what was listed in scripture. Those are qualities that you can bring to your marriage and use for the sake of each other. You need the quality of living with compassion — not for yourself, but for someone else. You need the quality of not just being kind to yourself, or patient with yourself, but learning to live, wanting to live, insisting on living as if the other were the only thing that matters. A humility and meekness that leads to a truly sacrificial way of living should be what you attain. When storms appear, you don't try to just get yourself safe, but you look to the needs of the other. In the face of risk, you need to risk losing yourself for the sake of the other. When you are threatened, you don't cover yourself alone, but you give and seek shelter together. None of that is easily done. In truth, we've all been taught, so carefully taught, to look out for the self that it's not always second-nature to look out for someone else. Even when we remember that the example Christ gave to us was a good one, an excellent one, a loving one, there are those moments when it seems too difficult to love, to care, to sustain, to keep safe, to work hard. How many people, despite the predictions, the forecasts, and the warnings in life, when the winds come and the waves too, only when the trouble is worst finally realize they should have done more? But I tell you, do not look for something to save you when the trouble is at hand. Make preparation while the time is still good. Then you can let the peace of Christ rule in your hearts — a peace that comes about because you know what you need, even before you need it fully. The scripture today said it: bear with each other, forgive each other, love each other.

Certainly, you'll love each other. That's why we're here today — to hear you say that you intend to keep on loving each other as much as you have already. Good for you. Accept our congratulations. But understand that loving each other as much as you already have won't always be enough. Rather, love each other more than you already have, more than you can ever imagine, taking what is contained in your preparedness kit and checking it, honing it, using it in good times and in bad. Take care to use compassion, kindness, humility, meekness, patience, forgiveness, and the love that binds it all together in perfect harmony.

The two of you are not strangers to the beach. Do not let yourselves be strangers to the word of God either, to the promise of Christ, to the example of your families, or to the love which each of you can have for the other, so that the winds may be favorable and the seas calm, and your life together will be blessed.

Traveling Like The Murdochs

Colossians 3:12-17 – *As God's chosen ones, holy and beloved, clothe yourselves with compassion, kindness, humility, meekness, and patience. Bear with one another and, if anyone has a complaint against another, forgive each other; just as the Lord has forgiven you, so you also must forgive. Above all, clothe yourselves with love, which binds everything together in perfect harmony. And let the peace of Christ rule in your hearts, to which indeed you were called in the one body. And be thankful. Let the word of Christ dwell in you richly; teach and admonish one another in all wisdom; and with gratitude in your hearts sing psalms, hymns, and spiritual songs to God. And whatever you do, in word or deed, do everything in the name of the Lord Jesus, giving thanks to God the Father through him.*

History doesn't record whose idea it was. But whether he or she suggested it, almost a century ago, Mr. and Mrs. Jacob Murdoch and their children piled into their Packard automobile and set off on a cross-country trip. Back then, it was both an interesting idea and something considered risky. I'm sure a few people even labeled it foolhardy. But once Mr. and Mrs. Jacob Murdoch had made up their mind, there was no stopping them. It didn't matter that they would be off road as much as on, that in some places there were no roads, that tires would burst and engines would overheat. It didn't matter that they would have to endure every known climatic condition, and some unknown ones as well. It didn't matter that they would use up days and then weeks until they accomplished their goal. What did matter is that they decided together to do something they wanted to do. But can you imagine all of them together in that car for 32 days? In comparison, you two might have it easy.

I hope you see the comparison. I hope you see that the two of you have decided to set out on a long trip knowing full well that the route is not always known, that there are hazards along the way, that other people have thoughts about the matter, and that too much togetherness will test anyone. And that doesn't even count the number of times that someone says, *Are we there yet?*

It's an interesting question. *Are we there yet?* There are at least two kinds of people in this world: those who figure that a trip is something that aims for a destination, and those who see that the destination of the trip is wherever you are. Who see not what will become, but what already is. So you will have to decide for yourselves — whether marriage is a destination or a trip. I hold for the latter, because I know that the question "are we there yet" can be something full of delight. Not just because of what you see along the way, but because of who goes with you.

I'm sure the Murdochs' car was packed. When you set out on a journey without knowing what might be, you have to be prepared for everything that might be. And some people do in fact pack it all. How much have you packed for your life together? Do you bring something for everything, for every time — or just the necessities? And what is a necessity? Allegorically, we could spend all day listing things. What is necessary on a trip, what is necessary in life? For me, maybe most of all, a map comes to mind. That's too structured for some people, but if you don't know where you started and aren't sure where you'll finish, and don't have much sense of where you are, where are you really? Romantics say, *Wherever we are is fine.* I still like a map. And do I stretch too much to suggest that scripture is such a guide. It was you, not I, who chose today's lessons.

You have to wonder how the Murdoch family spent their time while driving every day. I wonder if they pulled out the family Bible and read from the second lesson chosen for today, that reading from the letter to the Colossians. Especially the portion that says, *"As God's chosen ones, holy and beloved, clothe yourselves with compassion, kindness, humility, meekness, and patience."* You know, when you're cooped up together, and the hazards of life begin to pile up, when you face decisions about where to go and what to do, how to do it and for how long, when the days get long and you wonder whose idea this was, that's a pretty good reading to remember. Remember that there's a need for compassion, kindness, humility, meekness, and patience. Most people think of patience first, wondering to themselves how long they're supposed to put up with those around them. But it's not patience that's listed first; it's compassion. One should be able to put one's self in someone else's place and to care, a lot. One should be willing to overlook other people's grumpiness when they're tired, or their frustration when they're confused, or their disappointment at what didn't work out. One should realize that there's only one driver in the car, but to see one's self less as the leader in charge and more as the chauffeur in service.

It's the way the church sees our Lord too. Being God, he had every right to be in charge, to command, to demand, to always sit in the driver's seat. But we know he gave up some of that in our favor, showing us that love can never be commanded but can always be taken up. Kindness, humility, and meekness are the best baggage for any trip. Sacrifice is a virtue, not a burden. And love, in the end, is thankful.

Having left Los Angeles 32 days before, Mr. and Mrs. Jacob Murdoch arrived in New York on this date, April 24, 1908. There probably aren't a hundred people today who know that, or care. But the Murdochs knew and cared, and so can you — for the example they gave, of deciding, traveling, loving, dreaming, and accomplishing.

Through all the days of your journey together, may you be filled with a sense of accomplishment, that you did it, and a sense of joy, that you'd like to do it again.

Making A List, Checking It Twice

Colossians 3:12-17 – *As God's chosen ones, holy and beloved, clothe yourselves with compassion, kindness, humility, meekness, and patience. Bear with one another and, if anyone has a complaint against another, forgive each other; just as the Lord has forgiven you, so you also must forgive. Above all, clothe yourselves with love, which binds everything together in perfect harmony. And let the peace of Christ rule in your hearts, to which indeed you were called in the one body. And be thankful. Let the word of Christ dwell in you richly; teach and admonish one another in all wisdom; and with gratitude in your hearts sing psalms, hymns, and spiritual songs to God. And whatever you do, in word or deed, do everything in the name of the Lord Jesus, giving thanks to God the Father through him.*

Today is June 26. Yesterday was June 25. That means it's only six months until you celebrate your first Christmas as husband and wife. I wonder if have you finished your shopping yet. Now, you may think that I'm rushing things a bit, but in fact, some people would say that the success of a marriage has to do with how well he and she plan together and, more importantly, how well they shop together. And, as I say, Christmas is coming. What's on your list? What have you planned?

My mother was a person who always planned for Christmas. In her head, if not on paper, she kept a list of what any of us needed, whether we realized we needed it or not. On Christmas Day, I might get a pair of dark socks and I'd have to think, *when did I say I needed a pair of dark socks?* I could never deny that I said I needed them, because my mother and her list were never wrong. Could you keep such a list? Such a caring and careful list? Week after week, month after month, paying such close attention to each other that your needs and desires are not only noted, but fulfilled? Of course you could, but I daresay you won't unless you see the necessity of a particular gift and the value of a particular gift and the staying power of a particular gift, whether or not the gift has been asked for.

In truth, by choosing the scripture lesson I just read, you made a pretty good list of what the two of you should get for Christmas. The Bible says you two need compassion, kindness, humility, gentleness, and patience. But, being decent people, you probably think you have those in your possession already. And maybe you do. I already had some dark socks, but people who update their wardrobes every year and their computer systems every couple of years really ought to update their personal needs list too, if not in type, then by amount. Especially if you're not living by yourself and for yourself any more — now that the two of you are one.

I don't doubt you're generally compassionate people and you're surely gentle with each other as well and kind. But there's a mathematic situation to be dealt with here. Today, the two of you become one. The things you need to be able to live happily with each other multiply. One plus one becoming one will need at least twice as much gentleness, maybe three times as much humility, surely ten times more patience — and forgiveness too. You will both need lots and lots of forgiveness. You may say, admirable as all those qualities are, nice gifts that they may be, can we be sure that they're needed? Believe me, like the dark socks my mother bought me, they're needed. Maybe not exclaimed over when unwrapped, but so much appreciated and used when the need presents itself. Believe me when I say that the need for compassion, kindness, humility, gentleness, and patience will present itself. And how fortunate you will be, how delighted you will be, when the things you need are the things you have already.

The nice part about this type of gifts for Christmas is that you don't need to worry about size, color, or style. It all works for all of us. All you need to do is wrap them up — and the writer of scripture explained that too. "Over all these virtues," he wrote, "put on love which binds them all together in perfect unity." Put on a love which you have for each other. Let it be a love that has been modeled for you by people around you — a love that God gave to us first. Put on a love that is not envious, boastful, arrogant, or rude. Let it be a love that does not insist on its own way, that is not irritable or resentful, that does not rejoice in wrongdoing but rejoices in the right. Make it a love that bears all things, believes all things, hopes all things and endures all things. Strive for a love that never ends — a love that always looks for a way to give. Sometimes look for an awareness of the need for dark socks — sometimes the desire to give the gift of life itself.

Did you know that some people buy for other people a Christmas gift they'd really like to have themselves? It's true. But if for some reason you don't have these gifts in your possession already, ready for giving and sharing, I suggest you get shopping right away. Not because the marketplace will run out of them, but because I don't want the two of you to experience even a moment together without them. For no one ever said that you have to wait until Christmas to give gifts. Yesterday was June 25. Today is June 26. Tomorrow is, well, you get the idea. Day after day you have the opportunity to give gifts. Give gifts that you want, gifts that you need, gifts you can share, gifts that you'll cherish. Give gifts that will make every day of the rest of your life together, a Christmas. May it be so!

When The Wolf Huffs And Puffs

Matthew 7:24-29 – *Everyone then who hears these words of mine and acts on them will be like a wise man who built his house on rock. The rain fell, the floods came, and the winds blew and beat on that house, but it did not fall, because it had been founded on rock. And everyone who hears these words of mine and does not act on them will be like a foolish man who built his house on sand. The rain fell, and the floods came, and the winds blew and beat against that house, and it fell — and great was its fall!" Now when Jesus had finished saying these things, the crowds were astounded at his teaching, for he taught them as one having authority, and not as their scribes.*

When selecting scripture readings for their wedding, lots of brides and grooms choose verses dealing with love, commitment, and fidelity. You, on the other hand, chose something that reminds us of the three little pigs. That's not the way Saint Matthew wrote the story, but I suspect that more people know Mother Goose than Saint Matthew. I will tell you that there was a pig who built his house using straw. And there was a second pig who built his house with sticks, while the third pig used brick. Then the wolf came. The wolf who huffed and puffed and blew down the straw house. Who huffed and puffed and blew down the stick house. Who huffed and puffed — and huffed and puffed — and still couldn't do any damage to the house made out of brick.

What is the point of that story? Is it that brick houses are strong? Is it that some people build foolishly? Perhaps it is that the wolf is always around? All of that, I suppose. But what does that have to do with your wedding? Nothing — but it has everything to do with your marriage. There is a difference, you realize. Today is a wonderful day, a blessed day, a loving day, a remembered day. Today is the day of your wedding. But tomorrow is the day that starts your marriage. If the wolf seems absent today, watch out for tomorrow. It is not that I'm being negative, but that I'm being honest. Every life, lived singly or together, is confronted by wolves that huff and puff and threaten everything in front of them. The wolf may huff and puff anger or jealousy. The wolf may huff and puff poverty or inadequacy. The wolf may huff and puff conflict with your families or your friends. The wolf may huff and puff fear and sadness or even despair. It happens. I wish it didn't, but it does. Starting sooner than you could possibly imagine, the wolf will be at your door. And will you survive? Of course, you tell me, because you're smart people. You know the story of the three little pigs. You've even given up straw and sticks in favor of brick. But I tell you that even brick is at risk.

Unless you understand scripture, that is. Unless you see the difference between Mother Goose and Jesus the Christ, even brick is at risk. In her story, Mother Goose gave general advice: to build in strength so that the troubles of life are held at bay. In Saint Matthew's gospel, we hear a similar account: build on solid rock and not on sand. In the Bible, the reference to rock and sand has nothing to do with architecture, and everything to do with our relationship to Jesus. Jesus did not say build on rock and not sand. Rather, he said that anyone who listened to him, anyone who paid attention to him, anyone who obeyed him and put into practice what he said would already have the strong foundation that keeps the wolf away from the door. What is it that Jesus taught, that you should remember? He said, *You shall love the Lord your God with all your heart and mind and soul and strength. And you shall love your neighbor as yourself.* It's as simple as that. But it's also as difficult as that. For if you agree too readily to Jesus' words, if you always love God and humanity, you probably haven't fully understood the meaning of those words. For in truth, we forget to love God, and some days we don't even like the people around us. The two of you will have your problems too. More than once you will have to rebuild a life whose foundation wasn't strong enough. More than one marriage fell because of the sand. But your marriage can last if you remember that God who made you in the beginning and watched over you this far in life, promises from this time on to be your guide, your friend, your lover, your sanctuary, your architect, and your Savior. He will say to the wolves that will confront you every day, "*These are mine. They have heard my word and dwell richly in it. Let them alone. Let them to me.*" So that the peace which passes all understanding may keep your hearts and minds in Christ Jesus. Amen.

And Some People Like Beaches

Psalm 121 – *I lift up my eyes to the hills — from where will my help come? My help comes from the LORD, who made heaven and earth. He will not let your foot be moved; he who keeps you will not slumber. He who keeps Israel will neither slumber nor sleep. The LORD is your keeper; the LORD is your shade at your right hand. The sun shall not strike you by day, nor the moon by night. The LORD will keep you from all evil; he will keep your life. The LORD will keep your going out and your coming in from this time on and forevermore.*

Matthew 28:16-20 – *Now the eleven disciples went to Galilee, to the mountain to which Jesus had directed them. When they saw him, they worshiped him; but some doubted. And Jesus came and said to them, "All authority in heaven and on earth has been given to me. Go therefore and make disciples of all nations, baptizing them in the name of the Father and of the Son and of the Holy Spirit, and teaching them to obey everything that I have commanded you. And remember, I am with you always, to the end of the age."*

I have heard it said that there are some people who choose to spend their spare time, their vacations, in the mountains. In the dark, chilly, and rocky mountains. But I say that those are people to be pitied, especially when they could choose to spend their time at the beach. You two, more than most people, understand the goodness, the delight, the glory of the beach. It is truly a place where good things happen. And it's not just a place, but also an idea, an atmosphere, a way of life. For my wedding gift, I wish you long years together on a white, pure, bright, and sandy beach. That is my wish.

Unfortunately, it's not going to happen that way. You'll spend enough beach days together and most of them will be good. But not all of them will be good. The truth is that there will be tiresome days and quarrelsome days when the joy of marriage is forgotten and the stresses of life take over. There will be days when the sand on the beach burns your feet and gets irritatingly stuck in your suit. No, it won't always be perfect. Though you surely don't believe that right now; on their wedding day, very few brides and grooms believe that. But it's so — and the rest of us can testify to it. Not every beach, not every beach day, will be full of bright sand. Some will be covered with pebbles, stones, and rocks that tear at your feet and your dreams, at your hopes and your life. You will be tempted to give up.

The scripture lesson I just read reminds us of another time when it would have been easy to give up. Jesus had invited friends of his to be witnesses to his life and his work and his commandments. For a while, everything was good. But you know enough of the Jesus story to know that the good didn't last, and that evil took over, resulting in Jesus' crucifixion. It would have been easy for Jesus' friends to say, *It was good while it lasted, but it got really rocky at the end.* But God, not content to let rocks define life, raised Jesus from the dead and promised new life to all his followers. That means me — and you — and others here too. When life is rocky and when it's hard to walk on, when you're sure that only harsh pain is around, remember Easter and the promise of new life that turns rocks into sand and turns what is deadly into what can be lively and delightful again. Remember that rocks will become sand.

You can remember that because, being beach people, you already know how sand is created. You surely know that sand didn't start out as sand. It started out as pebbles and stones and rocks, all of which were tossed by the waves and tumbled on each other, smashing and cracking, all the while losing their sharp rockiness and more and more gaining their smooth sandiness. It will be that way in your life too. That there will be rocks, but they will always be becoming sand.

Though there will be some awful days when your impatience leads you to want the rocks to become sand right away. Sadly, it doesn't happen like that, simply because you're human beings with all the faults and troubles that means. With all the joy and promise too, but some days you may have to wait for the wrong to become right, for the lost to be found, for the sad to become happy, for the dark to become bright and for the rock to become sand. It may seem that it takes forever. But remember the Old Testament words in the psalm, that "the Lord will keep you from all evil; he will keep your life. The Lord will keep your going out and your coming in from this time on and forevermore." Jesus said to his friends, "No matter what lies ahead, 'Lo, I am with you always, to the end of the age.'" That is his wedding wish for you. I wish you a sandy beach life. He wishes you the knowledge that you're not alone during rocky times or sandy times. Your knowledge of that, your trust in that, your delight in that, could make all the difference. It should make all the difference. You will look at the sand and know where it came from, and be glad in it.

I have heard it said that some people like to spend their time in the mountains. But maybe they're not to be pitied. Maybe they just read a different scripture and hear a different sermon. But it's the same promise God makes to them as to you, and to us all, that he is with us always, in everything, even to the end of the age. Even to bright beaches beyond — that he is with us.

And We'll Hope It Gets Better

Psalm 100 – *Make a joyful noise to the Lord, all the earth. Worship the Lord with gladness; come into his presence with singing. Know that the Lord is God. It is he that made us, and we are his; we are his people, and the sheep of his pasture. Enter his gates with thanksgiving, and his courts with praise. Give thanks to him, bless his name. For the Lord is good; his steadfast love endures forever, and his faithfulness to all generations.*

July 2. What a special day and what a special day to get married. What a special day to celebrate, because July 2 is the birthday of our nation. Ooops — you've confused July 2 with July 4. You're too early; it's not time to celebrate yet. But you see, the agreement to the Declaration of Independence actually occurred on July 2, 1776. The business happened on July 2; the celebration came later on July 4. So both dates are connected to that historic moment that is newness and independence. That is what makes July 2 such a good day to get married. There's a change being made. There's an ending and a beginning. There's a celebration of it all, that surely goes on forever. Or so said the scriptures you chose for us today.

We heard in those lessons that when you enter into marriage, you leave some things behind, and grab hold of other things. You move from the old to the new. Maybe move from the certain to the scary, when you leave single-ness behind and move to double-ness. It is when you leave behind the family that was your parents in favor of the family that is you. But in declaring independence from some things, you pledge dependence on something else. You give up an emphasis on the self in order to delight in the other. You find strength in realizing that you can do and want to do together what you could not do alone. Though you value the past, you see more promise in the future. All that is what July 2 is about.

That is what the founding fathers realized too. Some things are done better together, not separately. Though the past was glorious, the future will be even finer. You always need to move on, making something new. Not that you get rid of all that was, but that you are committed to all that will be, and add to it as you go along, so that your life together will be like a rising sun.

In Philadelphia that fateful summer, during all the deliberations, George Washington sat in an ornately carved chair that had a half sun pictured on the back of it. Just looking at the chair, you couldn't tell if it was a setting sun or a rising sun. But when independence was finally proclaimed, Benjamin Franklin saw a strong, hopeful, and promise-filled future. He was happy to proclaim that it was surely a rising sun. So it was on July 2 then and there; so it is on this July 2 here and now. There's hope, promise, and celebration in the air and it's blessed by God. Not just a declaration of independence from, nor even just a declaration of dependence on. But that we pay attention to the theme of the other lesson which reminded us that you continue with each other and in partnership with the Lord God who is good, and whose steadfast love endures forever.

July 2. What a special day. What a special day to get married. What a special day for all of you to celebrate and then comes July 4!

Although the big day in Philadelphia was July 2, the celebration came on the July 4. That's when the good got better, when the original was amplified and finally celebrated. Even though Washington, Franklin, and the others thought they had it right on July 2, they realized it could be even better. In the same way you will realize that your marriage can and should get even better. You think things are good now? All of us gathered here wish you ever more, bigger, happier, greater, and lovelier times and things in the days and years ahead, always blessed by God who once called you into being and still calls you by name. We obey what the scripture said, and we "enter his gates with thanksgiving, and his courts with praise, giving thanks to him and blessing his name." Celebrating with you, twice. Once on the second and again on the fourth with bands and parades, with picnics and fireworks. And a prayer that you'll be glad in it all.

A Pirate Take-Away

Matthew 5:1-12 – *When Jesus saw the crowds, he went up the mountain; and after he sat down, his disciples came to him. Then he began to speak, and taught them, saying: "Blessed are the poor in spirit, for theirs is the kingdom of heaven. Blessed are those who mourn, for they will be comforted. Blessed are the meek, for they will inherit the earth. Blessed are those who hunger and thirst for righteousness, for they will be filled. Blessed are the merciful, for they will receive mercy. Blessed are the pure in heart, for they will see God. Blessed are the peacemakers, for they will be called children of God. Blessed are those who are persecuted for righteousness' sake, for theirs is the kingdom of heaven. Blessed are you when people revile you and persecute you and utter all kinds of evil against you falsely on my account. Rejoice and be glad, for your reward is great in heaven, for in the same way they persecuted the prophets who were before you.*

For your wedding today, you chose three scripture lessons. The first dealt with the joy of being a child of God. The second laid out some of what it means for one person to love another. The third reading is a list of what we call beatitudes. And they all begin in the same way: "Blessed are you when…." But "blessed" isn't the best English translation of the word. "Happy" is much better, more exact. So in his gospel, Saint Matthew reminded us that Jesus gave his followers all those examples of how and when to be happy. But there's one that he missed. The beatitude that says, "Blessed are you, happy are you, when you're a pirate."

Now, you and your friends may think that I'm making this up because I know of your love for and allegiance to East Carolina University and its buccaneer mascot. And they're right, to an extent, but there's more to it than swashbuckling football players. Knowing that a pirate is someone who takes something from someone else, in your marriage, I encourage the two of you to be pirates toward each other. Not stealing the good stuff, but taking away the bad. But how does that work out?

When you are a pirate for the other, when you make up your list of what you should take from the other, I'd suggest starting with fears.

If you're really in love with each other, it makes sense to me that you would want to take away each other's fears. They don't do anybody any good, and you'll be better off without them. And why not take away each other's pains? You probably can't get rid of them all, but you can make a good start, I'd say. Take away each other's worries too. You know you have them. You know you'd like to lose them. Let the pirate to whom you are married take them away. Let the other take away your grief. Especially right now, let the pirate who loves you take away everything that makes you cry. You'll be better off in the end. That's what it means to be a pirate.

You may say to me, isn't a pirate someone who takes away the good stuff like silver, gold, and jewels? Yes, and the person who has lost those things ends up poorer. But in this case, strangely enough, when the pirate takes from you the awful things, you end up richer. Can you imagine a life without fears and pains, without worries or grief? You probably can't imagine it, because it happens so rarely. It happens so rarely because we can't rid ourselves of those things, though having a pirate in the house helps. Nor is it a one-way street. For when you both are pirates, when you each take away from the other all that is awful, wrong, tiring, and troublesome, you end up with a life together that is fine.

Logically, you'll say to me, if you each take away the other's bad stuff, don't you both end up with the same amount of bad stuff you started with? Not if you act like pirates. Remember what pirates did with what they stole. They buried it. In some cases, they buried it so securely that they forgot where it was. And wouldn't that be a bonus? Not only has your bad stuff been taken away, but no one knows where it is. So how can it ever be dug up? Happy are you when you take away someone else's stuff, because your own stuff is being taken away too — forever.

If Jesus came back to earth right now, would he enroll at ECU? That I don't know. But I do know that as he has been a pirate for us, that as he has taken away all that would harm us and bother us; he has taken away all that would tear us down and tear us apart, so he asks us to follow his example and take away from each other. So may your football loyalties remind you of your marriage loyalties, and the love God has already shown to us all.

Give A Penny, Take A Penny

Matthew 10:29-31 – *Are not two sparrows sold for a penny? Yet not one of them will fall to the ground apart from your Father. And even the hairs of your head are all counted. So do not be afraid; you are of more value than many sparrows.*

I went to the corner store the other day, and the bill came to $3.01. As I passed four one-dollar bills to the cashier, she said, *Don't you have a penny?* No, I didn't, or else I would have used it. *No problem*, she said, *take mine*, pointing to the little saucer with some pennies in it. Take mine now, and maybe you can pay me back sometime. Or pay back somebody else some other time. You know, it's like give and take. You take right now and you give later on. Some folks give now, and take some other time. *Does that actually happen*, I asked? *Does it really work out? Pretty well*, she said. Pretty well.

Funny how much sermon you can get out of a penny. But what the cashier told me ought to work for your marriage too. You know — give and take. Sometimes you take what you need, what you don't have at the moment, and sometimes you give what you have more of, in excess. Exactly how that might work in your marriage I don't know. But the details don't matter so much as your awareness and your willingness to share. Be the ones who are not always talking, perhaps not always giving, but thinking about it and thinking about your marriage every time you see a penny.

You're hard pressed to see pennies that much anymore. It's as if they've become invisible. A lot of people won't even stoop to pick one up, if they see it lying right there in front of them. Pennies are, well, just pennies. They're worthless. You can't get much anymore for just a penny. Long ago you could buy two sparrows. That was the market rate in Jesus' day — two sparrows for a penny. Not that he was teaching an economics lesson in that tenth chapter of Matthew's gospel, rather, he was reminding you and all of us about the love of God. He was saying that if God watches over little sparrows, cheap as they are, how much more attention he will pay to you, the best of his creation. Isn't that nice to know? Isn't that a great present to get on this day — the knowledge that God knows you, cares about you, and watches over you? And he always will.

I mention all this penny stuff because, in my reading, I came across the fact that 51 years ago today, April 22, 1955, Congress declared that the words "In God We Trust" would henceforth be stamped on every penny. It's not much money. It's a whole lot of sermon. That even the smallest coin you have will always remind of God. God will look after you every day of your life together — that's the giving part — and ask that you trust in him no matter what — that's the taking part. Or, in reverse, that you give God your trust and you take his steadfast love. It's all written down there, on the penny. Nor is that a surprise to the two of you, for you have grown up with that message of God's grace. Here in this very place, you learned what it means to be children of God. Little sparrows have a worth almost uncountable.

If you'll remember the penny, if you understand that the little things really do matter, you will have learned that lesson. Not that the list in the first lesson was little, but that a little of what was listed can go a long way: Compassion, kindness, humility, meekness, patience. Be aware of what you give, what you get, how you share, and how you see it grow. A penny here, a penny there — and soon you're talking about real money. A little compassion here, a little patience there — and soon you're talking about real love and a marriage that is worth something. It will be a marriage that is worth something because the two of you are worth something.

Some marriages don't last very long because he and she argue over money — who makes it, who spends it, who needs it, who wastes it. From now on, you'll see money in a totally different way. You will see it as the vehicle that allows you to share your love with each other, a love that God gave to you first. It is a love he gave and you took, a love that you give, and take. It is not always counting, not always remembering, not keeping score, but knowing that as long as you have a penny, you have enough.

A penny, and from me to you, a saucer to put it in, as a sign of God's love to you and through you, and your continued trust in him, and each other.

Here's How You Keep In Touch

1 Corinthians 13 – *If I speak in the tongues of mortals and of angels, but do not have love, I am a noisy gong or a clanging cymbal. And if I have prophetic powers, and understand all mysteries and all knowledge, and if I have all faith, so as to remove mountains, but do not have love, I am nothing. If I give away all my possessions, and if I hand over my body so that I may boast, but do not have love, I gain nothing. Love is patient; love is kind; love is not envious or boastful or arrogant or rude. It does not insist on its own way; it is not irritable or resentful; it does not rejoice in wrongdoing, but rejoices in the truth. It bears all things, believes all things, hopes all things, endures all things. Love never ends. But as for prophecies, they will come to an end; as for tongues, they will cease; as for knowledge, it will come to an end. For we know only in part, and we prophesy only in part; but when the complete comes, the partial will come to an end. When I was a child, I spoke like a child, I thought like a child, I reasoned like a child; when I became an adult, I put an end to childish ways. For now we see in a mirror, dimly, but then we will see face to face. Now I know only in part; then I will know fully, even as I have been fully known. And now faith, hope, and love abide, these three; and the greatest of these is love.*

If you ever want to get in touch with me, you can call my home telephone number or my office number or my car phone number or my pager number. Or you can email me at my work address or either one of my two home addresses. You can do any of that. That doesn't mean that I'll respond to you. Isn't modern technology wonderful? It gives us lots of ways to do things, and lots of ways to *not* do things. Now, more than ever before, you have lots of places to leave a message that I may ignore. Please, just don't let that happen in your marriage.

Technology is fine, and some people are always thrilled with new ways to do things. I personally think the old ways have something to recommend them. Some people look at marriage and try what seems new and innovative. I personally think the old ways have something to recommend them. I mean, isn't marriage all about you loving each other? Were the old ways of saying that so bad? I'm stunned sometimes by the content of half the magazines on the rack today. They're full of new suggestions on how to keep the romance in your marriage. Was there something lacking in the old ways? Love is patient and kind. Love is not irritable or resentful. It does not rejoice in wrong, but rejoices in the right. Love never ends. That makes perfect sense to me. At least it's a sentiment that's been around for a while. Maybe we should add this one to it — that love keeps in touch. That's not a very romantic way to put it, I know, but if we're using the picture of technology here, remember that it's not enough simply to be able to leave a message. You actually have to do it. It's not enough to read about new or old ways to love. You actually have to do it.

Whether you get your suggestions for marriage from the Bible or a magazine, at least have the common sense to do what you should. Assuming, that is, that you know what you should do. I'm amused by the answering machine that in its entirety says: "Hi. I'm not here. You know what to do." Maybe I do — maybe not. It depends how much experience one has had. It depends who your teacher has been, and it depends whether or not you see the people around you as objects. It depends whether or not you have anything to say.

"Hi. You know what to do." Love each other as God has loved you: completely, unselfishly, eternally, and joyfully.

Some people leave messages on machines. Some people send messages with their eyes. Some people play games with their messages. Some people's messages are shared in a touch. There are lots of options, and what they share is a message that was given.

Are You Registered?

Psalm 128 – *Happy is everyone who fears the LORD, who walks in his ways. You shall eat the fruit of the labor of your hands; you shall be happy, and it shall go well with you. Your wife will be like a fruitful vine within your house; your children will be like olive shoots around your table. Thus shall the man be blessed who fears the LORD. The LORD bless you from Zion. May you see the prosperity of Jerusalem all the days of your life. May you see your children's children. Peace be upon Israel!*

The first question people ask about a bride and groom is usually about how they met. The second question usually asked is about whether I think it will last. The third question is whether or not they are registered. For those of you who haven't gotten with it yet, this whole matter of bridal registry is a chance for the couple to tell the world what they want us to give them as gifts. What they list may not be what they need, but, encouraged by some helpful department store personnel, it is certainly what they want. The printout for some brides and grooms goes on for pages. If you have managed to convince us that those gifts are what would make you happy, go for it, but don't confuse your wants with your needs. Be smart enough to know that what you really need doesn't appear on any store's computer screen. Psalm 128 got it right.

The psalm said that you're going to be content if you do what the Lord God wants. A family that lives with love, kindness, justice, patience, and humility has something of value even if they never possess any fine china. A bride and groom who have memories to share and more to spare are richer than any couple who collected silver and gold. A husband and wife who understand what peace is all about have a blessing beyond description. Remember that Psalm 128 closed with a blessing of peace.

It is not peace that means no fighting. In your life together, I expect you to disagree, for that shows the strength and wisdom of different points of view. It is not peace that means bending to the other's control just to end conflict. You are to be subservient only to God. It is not peace that is gray and empty of excitement. Make sure you paint your life together with the most vibrant of colors. It is also not peace that keeps an eye out for whatever attack might come next, but peace that says you have nothing to fear. After all, you are children of God. Peace is a gift from him — a gift of peace that the Bible defines as wholeness, in every way.

It's a wholeness that takes seriously the need for each of you to give in marriage. It is a wholeness that says a good life depends on more than things and a wholeness that connects the human with the divine. It is a wholeness that admits to joy and sorrow in life and understands that God walks with you through it all. It is a wholeness that realizes your life together is a gift from God. But on hearing the word "gift," there are some brides and grooms who get it all wrong. The purpose of this day is not to count up how much stuff you have received, but to see what and how many gifts you can offer. How much you can give to each other? How much you can give to your community? How much you can give to your families? Giving what you have first received, a kind of pass-through. What you have received, you should give.

Or, if you're going to keep it instead of passing it on, at least, make sure you send a thank-you note. Send a thank-you note that actually says something. Too many of us are tired of getting notes that say, "Thank you for the gift. It was a nice gift and we're glad we got it. You were kind to get us that." Do you know what's wrong with a note like that? I don't know if the couple liked what they got, or even knew what they got, let alone decided whether they would ever use what they got. The note didn't say anything. Some lives never say anything, either. But here is a good note: "Dear family, Thank you for giving us common sense, morality, and a place to live, for investing in our braces and our lessons, for coming to our recitals and our games, for allowing us to fall down, and for quickly picking us up. Thank you for the gifts of wisdom and hope and faith." You see, all those are gifts you have received, and none of them was on the register.

This was not registered either — that from God you have been given the gift of real life. Make sure you take care of it. If you know how to take care of your requested and registered wedding gifts, even more know how to care for God's free gift of his love for you. You do not care for it by putting it away in its wrappings, safe for some future time, though maybe forgotten. Care for the gift by using it every day. Care for it by making it something you need. Remember that there's sometimes a difference between wants and needs. Be wise enough to know the difference — and it is most wise to be certain that the gift of God you need is also something you want.

You'll get towels today, dishes, and lots of pretty things. You'll be glad for them all. But let your joy be greatest at this: that the love of God has come to you richly. We all pray he will grant you his peace forever.

Some Kleenex For When You Cry

1 Corinthians 13 – *If I speak in the tongues of mortals and of angels, but do not have love, I am a noisy gong or a clanging cymbal. And if I have prophetic powers, and understand all mysteries and all knowledge, and if I have all faith, so as to remove mountains, but do not have love, I am nothing. If I give away all my possessions, and if I hand over my body so that I may boast, but do not have love, I gain nothing. Love is patient; love is kind; love is not envious or boastful or arrogant or rude. It does not insist on its own way; it is not irritable or resentful; it does not rejoice in wrongdoing, but rejoices in the truth. It bears all things, believes all things, hopes all things, endures all things. Love never ends. But as for prophecies, they will come to an end; as for tongues, they will cease; as for knowledge, it will come to an end. For we know only in part, and we prophesy only in part; but when the complete comes, the partial will come to an end. When I was a child, I spoke like a child, I thought like a child, I reasoned like a child; when I became an adult, I put an end to childish ways. For now we see in a mirror, dimly, but then we will see face to face. Now I know only in part; then I will know fully, even as I have been fully known. And now faith, hope, and love abide, these three; and the greatest of these is love.*

According to Saint Paul in his first letter to the Corinthians, love is patient and kind. It bears all things, believes all things, hopes all things, and endures all things. Love supplies the kleenex. Actually, Saint Paul didn't say that last part about the kleenex. Because Saint Paul knew about love, he must have known how easily we cry. Isn't that wonderful! Can you imagine anyone being so insensitive as <u>not</u> to cry? Someone might insist that this is a happy time. Why would you cry? Because it <u>is</u> a happy day, why wouldn't we cry? This is a pledge you could make to each other, that because I love you, I will cry.

We did a study some time back and found out that there are something like seventeen different reasons people cry. There is physical pain, of course, but also fatigue, homesickness, embarrassment, and patriotism. They're all causes for tears. Some people cry with no effort at all. Some people need lots of encouragement. Some people are so sensitive that they can tell when the one they love is about to cry, before it even happens. Some people aren't very concerned even when the one they love can't <u>stop</u> crying. Some people are good at guessing the reason people cry. Some people don't have a clue. Some people are good at crying; others are not. This is a pledge you could make to each other: *Because I love you, I will cry.*

Some people in their relationships cry about each other. I'm not sure that's a good idea. If you cry about each other, I'm guessing there's some disappointment there, maybe some pain. That's the part of relationships that Saint Paul wanted people to avoid when he wrote that love is not jealous or boastful, that it should not be not arrogant or rude. If you're able, try not to cry about each other. And really, try not to cry for each other. If you cry for each other, there's a certain pity, a hint of insufficiency, some suspicion that the other person doesn't quite measure up. That's the kind of crying that speaks of irritability or resentfulness — a long list of what you did that you shouldn't have done, or didn't do when you should have. If I had my way, you wouldn't cry about each other and you wouldn't cry *for* each other. But I hope you will always cry with each other. This is a pledge you could make to each other: Because I love you, I will cry.

I will cry because I can't replace you and even if I could, why would I want to? I will cry because not every day will be perfect and not every dream will be fulfilled; I will cry because life is scary but because I know you are near me, I will cry tears of relief. I will cry because I understand what we have to give, how we fit, how I need you, and how you need me. I will cry because you make me laugh, and I realize how fortunate I am. I will cry because you remind me of other people who loved me, who in their own special ways brought me to this day. Most of all, it's the joy — always the joy. It only happens to a few people that they are able to say to each other that they are so happy, they can't stop crying. This is a pledge you could make to each other: *Because I love you, I will cry.*

If that is so for the two of you, think how much more it is true of God who oversaw your creation, your growth, your discovery, and your love. From him also come tears of delight, hope, and joy. You are his creation, the delight of his hand. Won't he give you what we ask? Did we sing the hymn only because we were supposed to? Was it not a fervent prayer we raised: "Give them joy to lighten sorrow. Give them hope to brighten life." That means we want you to know happy tears, not sad. "Go with them to face the morrow. Stay with them in every strife." That means we'll cry with regret whenever you go off; and we'll cry with delight whenever you come home.

The gifts from God are faith, hope, and love. Those three abide and Saint Paul said the greatest of them is love. I guess he's right. That's why you're here. At your promises, you cry because you love each other. But this is the pledge God makes to you, that because he loves you, he too will cry. Now, may the God of hope fill you with all joy and peace in believing, so that by the power of the Holy Spirit you may abound in hope — in love — and in tears. Amen.

Who's Keeping Score?

1 Corinthians 13 – *If I speak in the tongues of mortals and of angels, but do not have love, I am a noisy gong or a clanging cymbal. And if I have prophetic powers, and understand all mysteries and all knowledge, and if I have all faith, so as to remove mountains, but do not have love, I am nothing. If I give away all my possessions, and if I hand over my body so that I may boast, but do not have love, I gain nothing. Love is patient; love is kind; love is not envious or boastful or arrogant or rude. It does not insist on its own way; it is not irritable or resentful; it does not rejoice in wrongdoing, but rejoices in the truth. It bears all things, believes all things, hopes all things, endures all things. Love never ends. But as for prophecies, they will come to an end; as for tongues, they will cease; as for knowledge, it will come to an end. For we know only in part, and we prophesy only in part; but when the complete comes, the partial will come to an end. When I was a child, I spoke like a child, I thought like a child, I reasoned like a child; when I became an adult, I put an end to childish ways. For now we see in a mirror, dimly, but then we will see face to face. Now I know only in part; then I will know fully, even as I have been fully known. And now faith, hope, and love abide, these three; and the greatest of these is love.*

In chapter thirteen of his first letter to the church at Corinth, Saint Paul wrote these words: *Love is patient and kind; love is not jealous or boastful; it is not irritable or resentful. Love does not keep score.* Actually, Paul didn't write that last part, but that's certainly what he meant. Love doesn't keep score. Although he was writing to church members, referring to their affection for each other, Paul's words just as much apply to anyone embarking on marriage. Don't keep score, for in keeping score, the very thing that seems so important becomes nothing at all. Despite what it may seem, when people keep score, there is no winner. When one says he or she gave more to the relationship than the other, that's keeping score. When one say he or she caused most of the arguments, that's keeping score. When one says he or she cried more than the other did, that's keeping score. When one says that he or she forgot what the other thought one should have remembered, that's keeping score. Keeping score isn't what marriage is about. Despite what people think, competitiveness rarely brings a victory but often causes a defeat.

Still, if it is your make-up to compete, try to out-do each other in compassion, in humility, in patience, and in serving. In your marriage to each other, try to lose. That's the opposite of what the world says and of what your friends might advise or what your ego tells you to do. But it's not the world, your friends, or your ego that should determine your relationship with each other. Instead, as a model, I suggest the example of Jesus Christ. You'd be amazed at how many marriages begin without some reference to him, but I can hardly ignore the fact that we're just weeks away from Easter, the day Jesus was raised from the dead. If we're that close to Easter, we're even a bit closer to Good Friday, the day Jesus died on the cross. Talk about losing. We really should talk about it, for his example of sacrifice is something you can copy, if you will. Like him, you can be nothing. You can be a zero. You can be l'oeuf.

My French is atrocious, but my dictionary works. And I learned a long time ago that the French words *l'oeuf* refer to an egg. An egg is shaped like a zero. Zero means nothing. That is why tennis players like yourself use it in keeping score. *L'oeuf.* — nothing at all. In English, we say *love*. In tennis, you don't want *love*. But in your marriage, you should work hard to have it everywhere. Not simply love that is romantic, love that is exciting, love that is participatory, or love that endures, but love that is zero. It should be a love that tries to empty the self in favor of another.

You're church people. Do you remember the great New Testament passage that says: "Let the same mind be in you that was in Christ Jesus, who, though he was in the form of God, did not regard equality with God as something to be exploited, but emptied himself, taking the form of a slave, being born in human likeness. And being found in human form, he humbled himself and became obedient to the point of death — even death on a cross"? Some people see that as a zero. They see it that Jesus lost but we all won. It's upside down, isn't it? The more you give away, the more you have. The more you lose, the more you gain. How will people see your marriage and your own participation in it? Will they see you as a winner? Will they see that your winning comes about through losing? That will be difficult; for it may well be that it's harder to lose than it is to win. It may be harder to give away than it is to accumulate. But this is the real *l'oeuf* — that those whom God has joined together become less than they were apart from each other. It's the mathematics of matrimony. Some people say that one plus one equals two. And here you are. Some people say that one plus one equals one — and that is your new single life together. But I say that one plus one equals zero, if you'll do it the right way. If you'll see marriage as sacrifice, as emptying, as humbling, as pouring out for the sake of each other, you will know what *l'oeuf* is all about.

May you find richness in poverty and gain in loss plus joy in serving each other through all the days ahead.

Are You Really Sure About This?

John 2:1-11 – *On the third day there was a wedding in Cana of Galilee, and the mother of Jesus was there. Jesus and his disciples had also been invited to the wedding. When the wine gave out, the mother of Jesus said to him, 'They have no wine.' And Jesus said to her, 'Woman, what concern is that to you and to me? My hour has not yet come.' His mother said to the servants, 'Do whatever he tells you.' Now standing there were six stone water-jars for the Jewish rites of purification, each holding twenty or thirty gallons. Jesus said to them, 'Fill the jars with water.' And they filled them up to the brim. He said to them, 'Now draw some out, and take it to the chief steward.' So they took it. When the steward tasted the water that had become wine, and did not know where it came from (though the servants who had drawn the water knew), the steward called the bridegroom and said to him, 'Everyone serves the good wine first, and then the inferior wine after the guests have become drunk. But you have kept the good wine until now.' Jesus did this, the first of his signs, in Cana of Galilee, and revealed his glory; and his disciples believed in him.*

It will surely come as no surprise to the two of you that the rest of us have some questions about your future together. Basically it is this: *Can a girl with Carolina roots find happiness with a boy from Michigan?* But it's more than that, you realize. Some of us wonder if a boy who likes to hunt can be content with a girl who remembers Bambi. What about this one: *Can a girl who rides the train be happy in the front seat of a pick-up truck? Can a boy who eats kielbasa ever fully understand barbecue?* What about your differing views on country music, cats, chocolate, and wind chill? These are hard questions, and the way they are answered says something about your future. Some people, hearing those difficult questions, might suggest that there's no way any of it is going to work out. In addition to all the others, there is this one further question, your response to which will make all the difference with the rest. *Can water be turned into wine?* Because if water can be turned into wine, if something that seems that impossible becomes a reality, then we can have every hope for the two of you.

You remember the story. It's the first of Jesus' miracles and for me, the favorite. Jesus and his friends were at a wedding reception. That they were invited guests is vitally important, I'd say, for as you have invited to your ceremony the people you love and who love you, so we all can be glad that Jesus was included. But a snag developed. With all the preparations for the big day, it happens. And with a wedding reception that might have lasted seven days, it's to be expected that halfway through the event, the wine gave out. No wine, no party. No party, no joy. No joy — well, it was too much to consider. It was too much for anyone to consider. Mary hissed at her son to do something. And he did. They didn't tell us how he did it, because how he did it wasn't as important as what he did. But right from the beginning of his ministry, he showed how he would be. In the process, he showed us how life could be. He turned water into wine.

Would the couple who were married in Cana that day be just as married if Jesus hadn't been present, if he hadn't turned water into wine? Yes, they would. Without him, however, they might have lacked that extra "something" that a family enjoys when the joyful, active, and loving presence of Jesus is invited, understood, and loved. Can you see that presence and example of Jesus as an integral part of your life together? Do you see how he changes things?

Let's run this list:

You may not approve of each other's food choices or pet preferences, but surely you can understand sacrifice the way Jesus worked it out. When you're convinced you are right, you're still humble enough to see the rightness of the other, and that with Jesus there is an example of love, even when love doesn't always get returned. You may not know everything about each other's life stories, but you know enough to let all your experiences be clothed with morality as Jesus taught it. You may come from different backgrounds but you can appreciate that it all can be rooted in his giving of real and true life. Although you have different favorites in lots of things, Jesus' example reminds you of the joy of sharing all of them with each other, because your love for each other causes you to work to forge two into one. When you're tempted to go your own way, you can be reminded that since Jesus holds both your hands, there is only one way to go. But going out of your way for the other is probably the best way, since that's the example he gave us, even something of servanthood.

Don't be content to wait for times when caring and compassion might be called for but instead search out every way in which you can serve and love. Keep on loving, in spite of the risks — there are risks. It's foolish to imagine that the two of you or any couple of us would succeed. It might seem impossible that you who come from such different places might find success in your life together. Clearly, it would take a miracle but that is just what we're given. He who turned water into wine will turn your questions into certainty and turn your separateness into togetherness. He will turn your today into always — what the marriage ceremony calls a wedding feast that has no end.

At the wedding at Cana in Galilee, Jesus transformed water into wine and caused great joy to break out. May his presence at your wedding this day transform you into something more and better, much more and much better, that your love may overflow and your joy may never run dry.

Another Christmas Gift!
How Grand!

1 Corinthians 13 – *If I speak in the tongues of mortals and of angels, but do not have love, I am a noisy gong or a clanging cymbal. And if I have prophetic powers, and understand all mysteries and all knowledge, and if I have all faith, so as to remove mountains, but do not have love, I am nothing. If I give away all my possessions, and if I hand over my body so that I may boast, but do not have love, I gain nothing. Love is patient; love is kind; love is not envious or boastful or arrogant or rude. It does not insist on its own way; it is not irritable or resentful; it does not rejoice in wrongdoing, but rejoices in the truth. It bears all things, believes all things, hopes all things, endures all things. Love never ends. But as for prophecies, they will come to an end; as for tongues, they will cease; as for knowledge, it will come to an end. For we know only in part, and we prophesy only in part; but when the complete comes, the partial will come to an end. When I was a child, I spoke like a child, I thought like a child, I reasoned like a child; when I became an adult, I put an end to childish ways. For now we see in a mirror, dimly, but then we will see face to face. Now I know only in part; then I will know fully, even as I have been fully known. And now faith, hope, and love abide, these three; and the greatest of these is love.*

Have you noticed that the models in every holiday catalogue are smiling? Have you noticed that the kids on television commercials are always delighted with the toys they receive? Have you noticed that the snowy scene that graces the front of holiday CDs will probably never turn gray or slushy? I guess it's a perfect world after all. To be married this close to Christmas seems a double blessing. Perfection is the order of the day here too. If Christmas is perfect and your wedding is perfect, then your life will be perfect too. Right? Surely you're not fooled by the ads in magazines or on television. Christmas isn't always wonderful. For some people there are visions of sugar plum fairies and a dream that came true. But other people remember only the sadness, the disappointment of all that didn't happen as promised. Does that have something to do with expectations? Does it have to do with how we thought things would be or how things should have been? There's nothing wrong with dreams. How is it they sometimes turn into nightmares?

You realize that I've moved from Christmas to marriage. Is it always wonderful? We hope so, certainly. But there are pressures that threaten. Sometimes the pressure is from others, from outside. Sometimes the pressure is from us, from within. Sometimes it's obvious and sometimes it's unseen. But in marriage, there is often the terrible pressure that who we are and what we have must be perfect, in the same way that Christmas trees are always perfect, snow is always white, and presents are always appreciated. In the same way that the well-adjusted family sits around a fire that never goes out, singing carols that are always in tune. But here's a present for you, my gift to you early in the season. Don't worry about trying to match the expectations, trying to be perfect. Instead, concentrate on loving and being loved.

It is a two-part task, you see — to love and to be loved. Some people are good at being loved. They have become used to being the center of attention, and they'd be happy that the world revolved around them. These are the self-centered decision makers who take control of others' lives and who put forward expectations of perfection. They are the ones insisting that nothing else will do. But only being loved is not a good choice. You'd think that if being loved is wrong, then the better choice is to love but that can cause troubles too. A life that only gives and never receives will soon be as empty as a box the day after Christmas. There's something sad about people who delight in what once held something and now is good for nothing. I tell you that that marriage, that life, that family is best which knows how to love and be loved. A marriage, a life, and a family that understands that perfection is unreasonable may possibly block the best of all gifts — the grace of God.

That is what Christmas is all about. That is what your marriage should be all about, too. That when things go poorly — and they surely will — God will be beside you reminding you of the Christmas gift of Jesus who came with a forgiveness the world was unable to give itself. That's what the marriage ceremony means when it says, "Because of sin, our age-old rebellion, the gladness of marriage can be overcast and the gift of the family can become a burden." That's what scripture means when it says that love is patient and kind, not jealous or boastful, not irritable or rude. Love is not perfect. In fact, love exists because of imperfection. Were it not for sin, there would have been no need for Christmas. Were it not for the way we live, there would have been no need for grace. But what delights us today is that we are loved. In his richness, God has come to us as we are and announced that we are loved, and that he strengthens us to love each other. Husband and wife, parents and children, friends and neighbors — to love and to be loved — it comes as a gift. It comes like a wedding gift or a Christmas gift, all wrapped up in one. How fortunate you are to get it.

Just remember to unwrap the present and open what you have been given. In their excitement to see how much of their gift registry has been claimed, in their delight of discovering how many things they have accumulated, some brides and grooms forget from whom comes the best gift of all. And forgetting that they have received it, they forget to open it. If perchance they open it, some forget to use it. But to those who receive it, open it, and use it comes a blessing unlike anything else you will ever know.

Does that mean all your marriage will be perfect and no dreams will become nightmares? No, but that he who was a gift for the world will be a gift for you, that your love will be strengthened and your rest will be sweet.

When You've Each Always Done It That Way

1 Corinthians 13 – *If I speak in the tongues of mortals and of angels, but do not have love, I am a noisy gong or a clanging cymbal. And if I have prophetic powers, and understand all mysteries and all knowledge, and if I have all faith, so as to remove mountains, but do not have love, I am nothing. If I give away all my possessions, and if I hand over my body so that I may boast, but do not have love, I gain nothing. Love is patient; love is kind; love is not envious or boastful or arrogant or rude. It does not insist on its own way; it is not irritable or resentful; it does not rejoice in wrongdoing, but rejoices in the truth. It bears all things, believes all things, hopes all things, endures all things. Love never ends. But as for prophecies, they will come to an end; as for tongues, they will cease; as for knowledge, it will come to an end. For we know only in part, and we prophesy only in part; but when the complete comes, the partial will come to an end. When I was a child, I spoke like a child, I thought like a child, I reasoned like a child; when I became an adult, I put an end to childish ways. For now we see in a mirror, dimly, but then we will see face to face. Now I know only in part; then I will know fully, even as I have been fully known. And now faith, hope, and love abide, these three; and the greatest of these is love.*

No matter how certain you are of the love you have for each other, no matter how much your friends have given their approval or advice, no matter how much premarital counseling you have undergone, there's really no way to predict the success of your marriage, until the two of you decide what kind of Christmas tree you will have.

Anticipating that the decision may not be easy, it would be simple enough to determine from the outset that you will have two trees, or none at all. That seems a clever way to by-pass some kind of conflict, but all you've done is put off the inevitable. If it happens that she wants something real and fresh and green, something that smells like a tree and he thinks aluminum is nice, or something plastic that looks like a tree there will be a conflict. Maybe she prefers something small that sits on a table and he knows that a tree isn't really a tree until it grazes the ceiling. Perhaps she thinks several ornaments tastefully displayed are more than enough and he believes that every ornament ever made must be hung there with enough lights to please the utility company. Maybe she will say that this is what she has always done and he will insist that what he has always known is at least as correct. What shall we say is the right answer?

The right answer has nothing to do with what kind of tree or how big it is or how richly it is decorated, but it has everything to do with the season the tree represents. Or, if not the tree, then the presents. If not the presents, then perhaps the music. It happens sometimes that things get in the way of our focus. Christmas, for example, is not a holiday of the forest and green trees. Nor is it a spending spree. It is not a series of plays and performances. It's the birth of Jesus, the promise of God. Someone may say that I am rushing things. It's not Christmas yet. Can't you hold off on that sermon for a while? Not really, because the wedding is now. What should we say is the focus here? Is it rich appointments, beautiful music, the company of many friends, and the love of your families? There are other brides and grooms today who would gladly have any of that. But I wouldn't wish on them all of that unless they understand what marriage is all about.

Scripture says that love is patient and kind. It is not irritable or resentful, nor does it insist on its own way. We read that love believes and hopes all things and that it goes on forever. It involves the hard work of decision making and this is the greatest of all decisions: trying to determine what is the priority, what it's all about. I have known people who miss the truth of Christmas because they spent all their time baking cookies, making ornaments, and passionately choosing what kind of tree. All that is a part of Christmas but it's not really Christmas. Don't let that happen with your marriage and your life — that the details get in the way. There will always be details, but don't let the details get in the way or even take over.

Must the two of you always agree on what is detail and what is priority? It's nice, but not absolutely necessary, for surely you will not agree on the details, though you ought to agree on the priority. And this is the priority about which you should agree: that by your promises, you bind yourselves to each other as husband and wife. Agree that the bond you make lasts forever. Though there will be days the bond threatens to come undone, you will work hard to tie it up again.

When that is so, your love will be like the tree each of you wanted.

It will be fresh, green, and alive as she had wanted, but it will last forever as he had hoped. It will be small enough to fit everywhere and large enough to be seen by everyone. It will be decked with every kind of ornament, each of them just right, with all of them adding to the magnificence of your life together. It will have the light that will be dim for the quiet moments but turned bright for a joy inexpressible.

The choice is not to have two trees or none. It is not to have two concepts of marriage or none. The choice is that together you will share what you have and who you are; that the tree of this holiday season may be a symbol of the new life you now begin, blessed by the Christ whose new life gives meaning to this season and our whole life.

It's A Lot Like Gardens

Ephesians 5:31-33 – *For this reason a man will leave his father and mother and be joined to his wife, and the two will become one flesh. This is a great mystery, and I am applying it to Christ and the church. Each of you, however, should love his wife as himself, and a wife should respect her husband.*

One of the nicest things about Charleston is its gardens. Their beauty, charm, and graciousness is legendary. The only problem is that you can't see them, because so many times they're locked behind impenetrable gates. It's nice to know that there's something close by that's lovely, but if it's something that can't be enjoyed, what difference does it make? Some people would insist that I can do what I want with my property, and if I want to keep it private for my own enjoyment, I may do so. Other people believe that beauty should be available to anyone who wants to see it. Which should it be? Hidden or obvious? Public or private? Open or closed? I suggest that your marriage, like a Charleston garden, should be a bit of it all.

There will surely be private moments in your marriage — times of sharing and laughter, times of conflict and tears, that have nothing to do with the rest of us. That is as it should be. The Bible itself says that for this cause — marriage — a man and woman shall put away all that is around them, and hold tight only to each other. Then, you are right to guard your moments together, to carve out for yourselves a time and place of physical and emotional intimacy that's hidden behind some kind of gate. But don't stay behind that gate forever. Let your marriage be something public too, for you have received a gift from God that can inspire others. It's a gift that is yours, but it's not only yours. It's something held in trust for God. God has given you life — and each other. That's something to show off.

Sometimes people keep their gardens closed because they want nothing to spoil them. It is true that if you let people in, the fear is that they may trample off the path, pick the flowers, and topple the birdbath. But that's a fear that isn't often realized. How much better to delight in people and not worry about things, to show off what is lovely in your marriage, that the rest of us may thank God for his gifts. They are his gifts, something of his own creation. Lots of gardeners and lots of brides and grooms think that they themselves are solely responsible for all that is lovely. But isn't it true that all we do is arrange what God has given us first? It's not a work that originates with us, but it is a work that depends on us.

Despite what it seems, Charleston gardens did not spring to life full-blown and with total beauty. Sometime, there was a beginning. Sometime, there was nothing except the mind of God that said, *Here I will put something lovely*. Not that God planted a garden, but that God planted an idea and a promise. Today, the idea is that you should love each other forever. The promise is that he will love you that long too. In gardens and marriages, God gives us the raw materials and he asks us to present it beautifully. That means setting the boundaries, tracing the path, fertilizing the ground, arranging the blooms, and finding a focus. If you do all that, you'll have something to delight you when the gate is closed and something to delight us when it is open.

If you do it all of that well, shouldn't you always want the gate to be open? Like a Charleston garden, marriage can be a thing of beauty. In the years ahead, show off what is lovely. Show off what grows. Show off what was not made by you, but always is displayed by you. Show off the handiwork of God, what he has done, and what he has given. Show off the gift. It is a gift to be used, a gift to be maintained, and a gift to be displayed. It is the beauty that is your love.

Prepping For The Coming Storm

1 Corinthians 13 – *If I speak in the tongues of mortals and of angels, but do not have love, I am a noisy gong or a clanging cymbal. And if I have prophetic powers, and understand all mysteries and all knowledge, and if I have all faith, so as to remove mountains, but do not have love, I am nothing. If I give away all my possessions, and if I hand over my body so that I may boast, but do not have love, I gain nothing. Love is patient; love is kind; love is not envious or boastful or arrogant or rude. It does not insist on its own way; it is not irritable or resentful; it does not rejoice in wrongdoing, but rejoices in the truth. It bears all things, believes all things, hopes all things, endures all things. Love never ends. But as for prophecies, they will come to an end; as for tongues, they will cease; as for knowledge, it will come to an end. For we know only in part, and we prophesy only in part; but when the complete comes, the partial will come to an end. When I was a child, I spoke like a child, I thought like a child, I reasoned like a child; when I became an adult, I put an end to childish ways. For now we see in a mirror, dimly, but then we will see face to face. Now I know only in part; then I will know fully, even as I have been fully known. And now faith, hope, and love abide, these three; and the greatest of these is love.*

There's not a person here today who doesn't wish for you all the joys that life can bring. But at least a few people here today understand that it might not work out like that. The fact is that, no matter how much we would wish it otherwise, there are bumps in life that upset what we hope would be smooth. You know that too. You are no longer teenagers infatuated with puppy love and you realize the truth of the wedding ceremony when it speaks of "joys and sorrows and all that the years will bring." Not that you live with dread, but that you live with wisdom. You know what's most important to you when the storm comes.

We've had a series of storms this year, and more will surely come. Some of the storms have caused great destruction, some have been only threats. But in so many cases and in so many lives, people have been forced to examine what is theirs, and to assess what importance any of it has. It's a wonderful exercise for anyone, to ask — if I have to leave my house quickly, maybe leaving everything else behind to be ruined or lost, what would I take? Money is practical. Pictures are nostalgic. Clothing is necessary. What about medications or the family goldfish? What is the first thing you could grab? Each person's list is different from the others, but each person's list is instructive to the others, saying, *This is what I hold dear. Without this, I would be less and perhaps could not even exist.*

Do not just consider the physical stuff of life, but make an emotional list too. What must you keep, and what could be put away? If necessary, and maybe it always should be necessary, I could give up my success. I could give up my pride. I could give up my dreams. But I could not give up love, because like one scripture says *without love there's really nothing else left.* There is nothing of importance, that is. Faith, hope, and love, Saint Paul wrote, three big and important aspects of individual and shared life. But the greatest of these is love. The greatest is love for each other, love for the family, and love for the world around you. The greatest is love that is obvious, love kept inside, and love that is generous. It is love that is patient, love that is kind, and love that shares a burden. It is love that never stops — never ever stops. The nicest thing of all is that, when you have to go quickly, you don't have to spend time packing. Not if it's always close by, that is.

It is as close by as the love that God has always had for you. That's the kind of love, the amount of love, the reality of love to which I refer. The kind that you take with you just what you have received. The kind that you model your life on the example that is his. The kind where you live for the other more than the self, that you live in the future more than the past, that you give more than get, that you forgive and forget, and that, more than a bride and groom, you see yourselves as children of God. The kind where you allow that to make all the difference.

We do not wish storms for your life, but if there are storms, we wish for you the wisdom that knows how to love and the joy and strength and passion to live it.

Ah, The Classics!

Colossians 3:12-17 – *As God's chosen ones, holy and beloved, clothe yourselves with compassion, kindness, humility, meekness, and patience. Bear with one another and, if anyone has a complaint against another, forgive each other; just as the Lord has forgiven you, so you also must forgive. Above all, clothe yourselves with love, which binds everything together in perfect harmony. And let the peace of Christ rule in your hearts, to which indeed you were called in the one body. And be thankful. Let the word of Christ dwell in you richly; teach and admonish one another in all wisdom; and with gratitude in your hearts sing psalms, hymns, and spiritual songs to God. And whatever you do, in word or deed, do everything in the name of the Lord Jesus, giving thanks to God the Father through him.*

In my life to this point, I have never bungee-jumped. I have never had a tattoo or had my body pierced. I have never memorized the lyrics to any of Puffy Combs' songs. I suppose that some people would say I'm not with it. Some people might say I'm not very exciting. A lot of people would call me boring. Personally, I like to think of myself as classic and risk-free. I'll bet you think that's a good position for you to be in. Certainly, on this special day, you have chosen music from the masters. You have decided to wear clothing some people consider traditional. You have decided to include in our worship words that have stood the test of time in describing what makes a good relationship better. The New Testament letter to the Colossians said, "Clothe yourselves with compassion, kindness, humility, meekness, and patience." That is just fine with me. But understand, none of that is very risky. As if risk were a virtue. Maybe it is. Is risk the opposite of boredom? May I suggest that this be your risk — not that you bungee jump but that you give up living for yourselves and live for each other with those special qualities. Now that's something risky.

In truth, people today don't live much with compassion. It's a dog eat dog world, and we presume that personal power and strength is something to be prized. Compassion too often means pity, pity arises from scorn, and scorn is what follows defeat. But your marriage shouldn't be a contest. Except that you try to see which can outdo the other in showing love and in showing kindness that is more than courtesy. Kindness that starts inside and works its way out, kindness that is seen in service and service that is carried out sacrificially is what you should strive for. It is service that is done quietly, without notice or applause. That is a true picture of humility and a better picture of meekness than simply submission. No one expects that you will be submissive unless that means pointing away from the self to the other and pointing away from the two to the one, living together forever. And there's a risky word. Forever. Are there still people who marry with the intention of staying together forever or has matrimony become a convenience, something temporary? Is it something that fails because of a lack of patience? Patience fails because no one understands how to see forever. That is one definition of classic — that it lasts forever. Saint Paul wrote to the Christian church in Corinth, "Love endures forever," and he spoke on more than one level. So your love should last forever, because God's love for you has lasted that long too. Is that something classic, or just old?

There is a difference, I think, between classic and old. There are lots of things that are old — dinosaur bones, moldy books, faded grave stones — but they're not classic. To me, classic is something alive. Something that has been and is and will be. Something that has a history that stretches back and a promise that is poised to go forward. The love God has for his children comes quickly to my mind. Can we say that much about your love too? Perhaps, or maybe not. Maybe forever, or maybe today just beginning. It happens, you know, that classics do have a beginning; they have to start sometime. Bach and Handel didn't realize they were writing classics any more than Saint Paul realized he was writing the New Testament. It's only as things are used, appreciated, and repeated that they take on a life of their own. It's only as their worth becomes obvious and their purpose becomes important that they become classics. So may your life together be a classic. May it be that your love will be used and appreciated and valued — a classic. May your life have an obvious purpose — something classic. And may it be that your love, as an extension of God's own love, will endure forever — the most classic thing of all.

Go For The High Notes!

Psalm 98 – *O sing to the Lord a new song, for he has done marvelous things. His right hand and his holy arm have gotten him victory. The Lord has made known his victory; he has revealed his vindication in the sight of the nations. He has remembered his steadfast love and faithfulness to the house of Israel. All the ends of the earth have seen the victory of our God. Make a joyful noise to the Lord, all the earth; break forth into joyous song and sing praises. Sing praises to the Lord with the lyre, with the lyre and the sound of melody. With trumpets and the sound of the horn make a joyful noise before the King, the Lord. Let the sea roar, and all that fills it; the world and those who live in it. Let the floods clap their hands; let the hills sing together for joy at the presence of the Lord, for he is coming to judge the earth. He will judge the world with righteousness, and the people with equity.*

It happens to every vocalist sometime that, just when the performance is going along well, and the voice hits each note clearly and precisely, there suddenly appears in the score an F sharp three octaves above middle C, a note so high it could be sung only by the composer's imagination. Here is the singer's dilemma: *Do you go for it or not?* Balancing people's expectations against your own ability, do you try to reach that high note or not? Some people would vote for a conservative approach, suggesting choosing another note, or singing the offending note two octaves lower. Maybe even coughing at just the right moment. Why try for it and miss, they ask? Why screech and put us through mystery and misery — the mystery of whether you'll try and the misery that you did. Some people would say not to take the chance. But I say that in your marriage you should go for it.

You may wonder how I moved so quickly from music to marriage. But everyone knows it's an apt comparison. I maintain that music is noise arranged in a pleasing way. It's a bunch of random sounds that are brought together in a meaningful collection. Actually, in lots of meaningful collections. Some people take those notes and arrange them one way, while other people take the very same notes and arrange them in a different way. What some people put together is loud and showy; what others devise is lyrical and singable. Sometimes the way the notes come together is original and sometimes it's copied. But everyone is given the same sounds. Isn't it interesting what we do with them?

In marriage, we all get the same basic material. Marriage is a series of moments arranged in some particular way. Sometimes it's pleasing and sometimes it's not. Sometimes it follows other people's plans and sometimes it's uniquely you. But as is the case with music, so it is with marriage: that what is best is what is performed. Music, even beautiful music, that lies in the mind or on the page unsung and unplayed misses a lot. It is the same in marriage too. There's a difference between potential and performance, between what could be and what is. That marriage is best which takes a risk and tries for the high notes. In your marriage, go for it.

Of course it's a risk but is that so bad? Sometimes you'll reach, screech, and sometimes altogether miss what you tried for. Some people will say you failed and should have done something else. But anyone can hit the usual notes. How much more special it is to reach higher — and maybe to miss, but to say that you tried. There are some of us who would applaud your effort and encourage you to try again, because when you sing what you wanted and reach what you tried, when you take the risk and succeed, there is no sound more wonderful. In your marriage, go for it.

Go for what? Reach for what? Take what risk? Take the risk of loving each other — fully, when you don't have to, when it isn't convenient, when love isn't obvious in return. Take the risk of listening to each other — fully, even when what is said is unpleasant, when dissonance is more prevalent than harmony. Take the risk of learning when a solo is better than a duet and when it is not. Take the risk of knowing that for you, the ordinary is too ordinary, and the sublime is never ridiculous. In all things, going for the high note, and expecting to make it.

It's an acceptable risk, made even more acceptable because it mirrors the relationship God has with us. In music, in marriage, and in life itself, we are able to take the risk, because God takes a risk with us. Specifically, he promises us his blessing even before we ask. He who made us in the beginning is anxious to see what we'll do with it all — whether we'll sing alone or together, whether we'll sing a dirge or a ditty, whether we'll be content with the ordinary (which is all right) or whether we'll go for the high notes (which is exciting). Regardless of what we choose, he stays with us, and tells us to go for it.

That may be more than some around us are willing to give us. When we're asked to match God's perfect plan, when sometimes we miss it and sometimes we screech it, the world around us may wonder aloud why we even tried. Don't worry about it. Instead, know that when you go for the high note, when you reach beyond, whenever you try to match God's expectation and delight, the wonderful sound you hear is his applauding your taking the risk. What you hear is his applause and our own.

For the gift we give you today is our love, our encouragement, and our promise to delight in your love, when you sing the song, when you take the risk, and when you go for it.

It's All About The Timing

Ecclesiastes 3:1-8 – *For everything there is a season, and a time for every matter under heaven: a time to be born, and a time to die; a time to plant, and a time to pluck up what is planted; a time to kill, and a time to heal; a time to break down, and a time to build up; a time to weep, and a time to laugh; a time to mourn, and a time to dance; a time to throw away stones, and a time to gather stones together; a time to embrace, and a time to refrain from embracing; a time to seek, and a time to lose; a time to keep, and a time to throw away; a time to tear, and a time to sew; a time to keep silence, and a time to speak; a time to love, and a time to hate; a time for war, and a time for peace.*

There's a lot going on in central Virginia today. Aside from UVA's graduation in Charlottesville, over in New Market they're re-enacting the famous Civil War battle. There's an art show in Fredericksburg and a farm show in Leesburg. You can watch a rodeo in Oak Ridge or see classic cars at Douthat Lake. And there's your wedding. Not that your wedding in any way compares with those other events but all of us have chosen to be here, instead of there. We're glad about that.

Though, truth be told, there are some aspects of each of those other events that could have some impact on your marriage. Not impact your wedding, but your marriage. Think about the farm show in Leesburg. This time of year, the emphasis is on planting. Soon enough, another show will deal with the harvest. It's a matter of timing, isn't it? Which is what the scripture lesson said: that there's a time for everything, and wisdom knows when it is. There is a time to plant and a time to prune or rip up. Today, you're planting. We'll hope you never rip up. However, Ecclesiastes said there's a time to kill and a time to heal. Consider that Civil War battle. Each side just knew it was right, and was willing to fight to the death to prove its point. It's not a very healthy way to live, but we all know couples who have fought their share of battles. For some, it's a critical problem. For others, it's simply a different way of looking at things.

Like the art show in Fredericksburg — some people prefer one thing and some people prefer the other. Who is to say which side is the wiser? Maybe the wise person is the one who realizes how little is known. I'll bet some of those Charlottesville graduates think they're done today; the rest of us know it's all just beginning. Maybe you'll soon enough sigh with relief and say, that's over, thinking about the wedding. The rest of us will sigh and say that it's just starting — thinking about the marriage. Lee's parents know one aspect of that, since today is the thirty-fourth anniversary of their own marriage in this very place. Enduring, unchanging, timeless, lasting, like what's on display at the classic car show at Douthat Lake.

There's a lot going on in central Virginia today and a lot of it comes together in the promises you make to each other. Those are promises to love the other as you love yourself, to see the other's point of view, as your own point of view is seen, and to fight when the point is important, but to be wise enough to know that not many points are all that important. It is to know that what you begin today, if given half a chance, you can grow and become something classic. But it's all about timing.

The scripture said it: "For everything there is a season, and a time for every matter under heaven." Good stuff and bad stuff — daily stuff and eternal stuff. It is beautiful stuff and ugly stuff — your stuff and others' stuff. Likely, through the years, you'll experience it all. Some of it, we hope benefits you. Some of it, we hope matures you. Some of it, we hope humbles you. Some of it, we hope encourages you. But don't spend too much time on any of it, because there's always more to it than you may at first realize. In marriage especially, there's always more to it than you may at first realize.

This may be the kernel of it all: that to love and to be loved is the greatest joy on earth. Ecclesiastes didn't say it that way, but probably should have. Spend a part of each day loving, and a part of each day being loved. You have to do both. Lots of people think it would be wonderful if you would spend your whole day loving. But you'll be empty if you do, and you would not be as aware of what gift you have to give. Better to be loved, in turn. Better to be filled, to be completed, to even to be children of God. God loves us and wants us to love him back. God asks us to give to each other what he has first given us.

There's a lot going on in central Virginia today. A history lesson reminds us there's a time to be right, and a time to stop fighting. An art show reminds us there's always a time to see goodness in the way someone else sees things. A graduation we all know is more beginning than ending. A classic car show that brings back memories of what our own future one day will hold. That's a lot of stuff going on all at once. But the scripture said you have time for it all — that you have all the time in the world. And hopefully, you will have enough love to fill it all up.

We Wish For You: Flowers

John 13:34-35 – *I give you a new commandment, that you love one another. Just as I have loved you, you also should love one another. By this everyone will know that you are my disciples, if you have love for one another.*

Someone has already surely said to you that, for you, there will never ever again be a day quite like this one. Certainly, they're correct. But I'm not exactly sure what people mean by that. Are they saying that there will never again be a day when so many relatives and friends come to share some time with you? Or are they saying there will never again be a day when so many arrangements have to be made, causing this much fatigue? Or is it that there will never again be a day when you keep the daisies in one piece?

The reference there is to all the times people try to figure out their feelings for each other. More than one flower has given up its life in an attempt to help people figure out the truth of a relationship. From somewhere, those who were once a happy couple acquired a daisy and then started to pick it apart, petal by petal. He loves me, he loves me not. She loves me, she loves me not. On it goes until the flower is gone, along with the relationship. Really, if you have to wonder if you're loved, what kind of hope is there for the future? If you have to ask if you're loved, is there anything left?

In your wisdom, you have chosen a scripture lesson that encourages you to love each other. It's a scripture lesson you chose not because of some romantic factor, but because it tells the true foundation for the love you are encouraged to share. It doesn't say that you should simply love, but that you should love as a response to God's love. It says you should model your own loving, patience, and joy after that of God's. It says you should do to and for each other what God has done to and for you first. That is significant, understanding what God does, because God doesn't go around pulling off petals. The special flower that belongs to God has but one petal. Over it and about you, God says, I love them.

That's not to say that God doesn't get disappointed or that God doesn't get hurt. It isn't to say that God doesn't get frustrated or that God doesn't get upset in a major way. But having said over his flower's single petal, *I love them*, he chooses not to go further. No matter how many questions in life we may have about each other, it is inconceivable that God would *not* love us. This day, we all hope it's inconceivable that you would consider not loving each other. Like God, you may get disappointed, hurt, frustrated, and upset. It is, after all, the result of what we do and leave undone.

But if you think today is something wonderful, remember that the scripture spoke of an even more complete joy. A joy that comes about when you finally figure out just how you should love. You've made a good start but there are some among us who could tell you stories of what still can be. There are others who delight in their own love and wish for you something similar. There are yet others who remind you just how fully God loves and they ask you to try in some way to duplicate it. Let us be your mentors that we may pass on to you what was given to us.

That was part of the scripture too — that we should love in a manner that was passed on to us — as God has loved us, so we are asked to love each other. We're not to love because we're generous, because we're lovable, or even because we're obedient but because we've been loved already. Just how that might work out in your life I don't know. Right now, you're still sort of an unknown quantity. When you hold a daisy in your hand, you may be not quite certain whether to keep it or pick it apart, whether to delight in it or destroy it. But God says, *Delight in it.* Understand that what he has created is always something of beauty — a flower, a marriage, an eternity.

When you understand that, your joy will be complete. We wish for you flowers. We wish for you single petal flowers from God — and a love that, like his, endures forever.

Should Spelling Count?

Philippians 2:5-11 – *Let the same mind be in you that was in Christ Jesus, who, though he was in the form of God, did not regard equality with God as something to be exploited, but emptied himself, taking the form of a slave, being born in human likeness. And being found in human form, he humbled himself and became obedient to the point of death — even death on a cross. Therefore God also highly exalted him and gave him the name that is above every name, so that at the name of Jesus every knee should bend, in heaven and on earth and under the earth, and every tongue should confess that Jesus Christ is Lord, to the glory of God the Father.*

One of the most-asked questions these days does not deal with the existence of God, with the purpose of community, or with the meaning of life. Rather, the question on uncounted students' lips is: Does spelling count?

Of course it counts — or it ought to. Though in fact, the laziness or disinterest of our world has allowed it not to count — seeming to indicate that there is no need for standards or correctness, and that that good intentions are enough. But are they? A student can prepare a much footnoted treatise on a vitally-important topic, but if the spelling is wrong, and punctuation is ignored, if details are missing, the whole effort is called into question. Does spelling count? Why not? The Bible was right when it reminded us that a person who is faithful in a little is faithful in a lot, and that a person who is unfaithful in a little is unfaithful in a lot. The objection is raised that it's impossible to live in perfection but does that mean it's desirable to permit laziness? Laziness not just in spelling, but in marriage too — you want everything to be as right as it can be. In marriage, as in an assignment, if something is left out, the rest is less than it should be, and the whole effort is called into question. Your friends and family expect more than that from you. You should expect more from yourselves.

But you may fail. It happens in life that what we attempt is not what we reach, what we desire is not what we receive. There's a difference between striving and not attaining, and in not even bothering at all.

There's a difference between asking *before* the assignment is due, does spelling count, and in realizing sometime later on that an error was made. Fortunately, you have chosen to be married in the church that demands attention to details and announces forgiveness when the details are not met.

For — and it's an important reminder — *if* we leave something out, *when* we leave something out, even if you misspell terribly and punctuate rarely, even if marriage seems less than what models God's love, God is there to help with the corrections. Of all your guests today, he is the most important, though not every bride and groom take seriously God's promise to be present. God is not present to mark red F's on us and our misspelled lives, but he's quick to help us make corrections. He prefers that we do well in the first place, but when and where there are deficits, God will work to fix them.

The question "does spelling count?" is a question of both legalities and intention. Wondering about approval, we ask, "If I do everything the right way, will I be rewarded, or punished if I don't do it at all?" Assuming that there is some printed standard of what is acceptable and what is not, what "counts" and what does not, some people ask: *Do I have to kiss my spouse goodbye when I leave for work? Do I have to be as mannerly with my spouse as I am with strangers? Do I have to live every day as if it's our anniversary? Do I have to understand that sacrifice is something honorable and expected?* Yes, to all of that. Why not? Should we allow marriage to pass with a grade of 70, something far short of 100?

Sadly, that's precisely what happens — that we limp through marriage thinking that "good enough counts." But good enough isn't good enough, because the well-done finished product is so much more desirable. Saint Paul wrote, "Let the same mind be in you that was in Christ Jesus" who gave himself completely for those he loved. Who gave himself not half-heartedly but completely. In your life together, that means you're asked to pay attention to the details, consciously caring about what other people might avoid or dismiss. But don't get so bogged down in the details that you miss the joy of the whole picture. That's not contradictory — that's complete. It's a conscious decision on your part to know a complete joy and a complete love that models Jesus. He said in scripture, "This is my commandment, that you love another, that your joy may be full." That you love each other as he loved you first — with a sacrificial, complete, and eternal love that counts.

Maybe The Best Present Of All

Luke 1:78-80 – *By the tender mercy of our God, the dawn from on high will break upon us, to give light to those who sit in darkness and in the shadow of death, to guide our feet into the way of peace."*

The child grew and became strong in spirit, and he was in the wilderness until the day he appeared publicly to Israel.

We've finally gotten to this place and this moment. It's been a long time coming, but we're all delighted that you've made it. We're all delighted that you intend to be together for a long, long time. There's no reason to expect anything else. However, just to be sure that your relationship is secure, there's one more thing to do. You need to take the Autumn Compatibility Test.

My wife and I just got back from a week's trip to New England, taken specifically to see the fall colors. Soon enough, they'll be here too, with the countryside bursting forth in reds, yellows, and purples. But here's the test: when you see autumn at its most colorful, at the height of the fall season, how do you feel? Are you delighted to see the color, feel the coolness, and experience the vibrancy of it all? Do you look forward to every day this month brings, which is the absolute end to a too-hot summer? Are you instead depressed by the knowledge that every day this month gets us closer to a cold and dark winter? Do you see each colored tree as a testimony to death, knowing the ground will soon be piled high with dry and dusty leaves? Some people choose one thing, some people choose the other. In truth, there's something to be said about either choice. Each is a good choice. My point today is that you need to make sure that you don't suggest that your choice is the only choice. We all know people like that, don't we?

I have made a decision, and that's the way it's going to be. You may have an opinion of your own, but it doesn't really matter to me, because what I think and what I say is all that matters to me. Whether I like red and yellow leaves or hate them, whether you agree with me or not, is not the point. It's my life and I'll run it like I want. That may be all right if you're the only person living on earth. But on this day of your marriage, that's an attitude not at all acceptable. That is the point of the

Autumn Compatibility Test — that each choice is right, even that each point is best, and that each point needs to be considered. It's perfectly acceptable to see the beauty and color of each day and to rejoice in it, but not to be giddy about it, because there really is a time of darkness and pain ahead. Life isn't always bright, crisp, and refreshing. That's just the way it is. But understand that even when you're in the middle of darkness, pain, and signs of death all around, see that there's still a spring ahead. There is a new, fresh, life-giving time of hope. Can you apply that to your marriage? You can, but not to your wedding. Today is one day, and tomorrow it will be over. In your marriage, can you realize that you must look beyond a single day, on down the way? Your life together may be a pattern of happy day, dismal day, happy day, dismal day — or maybe two dismal days in a row followed by three happy days in a row. The order of it doesn't matter, but what you do with it matters a great deal. It matters what you do with your life and how you deal with each other. It especially matters when one of you is bright and the other is dark. It matters when one of you is hopeful and the other is depressed. It matters when one of you sees autumn as the end of summer and the other sees it as the beginning of winter or when one of you looks everywhere and sees beginnings and the other looks everywhere and sees endings. It is important to remember that marriage is a journey, not a moment — that is something whole, more than just a part. Also, remember that the promise of God's presence is there throughout. God who planted the trees and who arranged the colors, God who allows the cold darkness of old life and who promises the bright freshness of the new, promises to be with you too. He promises to be with you always.

Of all the presents you'll receive today, that's the best of them all.

Yes, It Can Be Scary

Genesis 12:1-3 – *Now the Lord said to Abram, "Go from your country and your kindred and your father's house to the land that I will show you. I will make of you a great nation, and I will bless you, and make your name great, so that you will be a blessing. I will bless those who bless you, and the one who curses you I will curse; and in you all the families of the earth shall be blessed."*

I'm sure you'd agree that Beaufort is a nice place for a wedding. In support of that, you could tell me about the scenery, the climate, and the accommodations. But did you ever consider how your marriage might be tied to Beaufort's history? I did not say your wedding, but your marriage.

You know already that Beaufort is an historic town, located on the eastern shore of the continent. That means that when passengers first traveled from England to America, they often stopped here. Sometimes they stayed here, sometimes they moved on. Those are the three different ways you and lots of other people look at marriage. Some people look back, think about where they came from, delight in having memories, and maybe even wish that things now would be as good as things were then. Other people say they can't live in the past, no matter how good the past was. They have to exist in the present — to live, love, and work in the here and now. Still other people would say that living in the present is nothing unless it points to the future. Planning for tomorrow and all the days afterward — that's how life is to be lived. Some people came to Beaufort but looked back to where they came from. Some people left the past behind and settled here in these very streets. Some other people pushed inland further and further.

Are you waiting for me to tell you which one is the right way to view your marriage? I won't do it, because I can't do it. There is no one right answer. Even if the two of you agree on the answer, it still may not be the right answer. In fact, when any of you has a quiet moment, you may ask your spouse if he or she tends to look back, stay in the present, or move on. Find out, and offer your answer in turn. Then, regardless of what either of you, what any of you, answers, remember the scripture

I read to you a few moments ago. It's one of the oldest in the Bible, already 4,000 years old. It's the story of a man and woman, Abraham and Sarah, who thought they heard God speak to them, thought they heard God direct them, were certain they heard God make a promise to them. Here was the promise: that as God had been one with them already, he would continue on with them in the days ahead. Fair enough. In fact, behind God's promise was the notion that he wanted Abraham and Sarah to follow him. He wanted them to leave their homeland and cross miles and miles of uncharted land. Some people think that's how marriage is — that the man and woman each leave their old homes, their old lives, behind and move across miles and years of what is uncharted. That is scary. Lots of people, old and young, can tell you that marriage is very, very scary. It does not always work out the way we first intend. But Abraham and Sarah and all their descendants can tell you that more important than the fright is the promise that God will be with you throughout. It's a promise that is everlasting.

When you look back, and sometimes you will, look back to see when it was and how it was that God took your hand. How he has been with you in the difficult, in the delightful, in the uncertain and on the day when you found each other. Look back, and see the promise of God, never to let you alone. While you live, love, and work through the present, slogging along in the details of every day, see that God is still a constant presence in your life. He may be overlooked sometimes or he may be consciously ignored sometimes, but he never ever drops out of your sight if you will look for him and see and hear his promise. When like Abraham and Sarah, you move on to whatever is next, know that the journey will be better, smoother, more secure, when you travel accompanied by God who is so full of promise.

Here we are in Beaufort, a town where some people once looked back across the sea, where some people settled in these very streets, where some people vow to move on into the future together. As that is you, may you remember that the God who made extravagant promises to Abraham and Sarah makes them to you as well, and vows this day and always to fulfill them.

The Rocks Become Sand

Psalm 139:1-3 – *O Lord, you have searched me and known me. You know when I sit down and when I rise up; you discern my thoughts from far away. You search out my path and my lying down, and are acquainted with all my ways.*

This beach didn't start out as sand, you know. Long ago there was rock here. There were lots of rocks here. But the waves came, the winds came, and the rocks were tossed, broken, washed, softened, and beaten again and again, until finally there was sand. But here is a question: Is sand still a rock? If it is, when did it stop being mostly a rock and more sand. Will it ever become just sand?

You may think you've wandered into a lecture on geology. But in truth, much of what we say about rocks we can say about the two of you. Long ago, like rocks, you were — and maybe you were even close to each other. But rocks, boulders, and stones don't always touch, rarely fit, hardly ever nestle. That distance from each other exists before there is turmoil. Maybe you think that the winds and waves that come, whatever tosses rocks around, is something that destroys. I say, not destroys, but changes. Life's troubles change rocks that were only close to each other into grains of sand that touch each other, nestle each other, and seem to be like each other.

Someone can ask if maybe it was better when each rock was an individual and looked only like itself — when there were big rocks and little rocks — when there were sharp rocks and smooth ones. Isn't it important to have a personality, something different than every other grain of sand? Perhaps it is. But remember the question: *is sand still a rock*? What does this all have to do with your life together?

Simply this — that you started off apart. Maybe you were close, but apart. Then came all that changed you. Some of it was gentle and washed over you, like an incoming tide. Some of it was windy, like a high category storm. Some of it was crashing and scary. Some of it made people hide — hide from each other and from themselves. Some of life's troubles were so bad you wondered if anything would survive. But rocks do survive. Rocks are changed, but they survive. Just as you have survived and will continue to survive. Not just because you have lived through the experiences that change rock into sand, but because as sand you are surrounded by grains just like you. You are surrounded by people who have also weathered the storms and been weathered by them. You are surrounded by people who know how you were, how you have been, and what you can be. These are people who touch you. Some of those people have watched the transformation are here today. There are surely others you've probably forgotten. But all of it is of God.

In the beginning, God... That's the way the scripture story is told. In the beginning, God... Maybe you think the story only refers to the earth and the story of creation. But the story of the creation of the earth is also the story of humanity. The story of humanity is your story too — and ours. In the beginning, there was rock, and God saw that it was good. But the rock became sand, and it was also good. You are good. Not perfect, not blameless, but good — and not good because of anything you have ever done, but good because God made you. Good because you are children of God and you will continue to be.

That is the other part of creation. Not simply that God made and then sat down or went away but that God who made this world and all that is in it continues through all of time to care for it. He continues to care for it and to care about it. If there is wind and wave that seems too harsh, God gives assurance that no rock, no person, no child of God is ever alone. You and every child of God is surrounded by God's love, and the sand that is community.

Hear again the words from the psalmist: "O Lord, you have searched me and you know me." "How precious to me are your thoughts, O God! How vast is the sum of them! Were I to count them, they would outnumber the grains of sand."

In some wedding ceremonies, two candles give their light to a third - and there's a powerful symbolism in that. You've chosen to take two jars of sand and combine them into a third. There's powerful symbolism there too. Each of you is now a part of the other, and that you together are now a part of all of us. You are a part of all of us who once were rock, all of us who have been through trials, all of us who were joined with others, all of us who lose ourselves in the wide expanse of God's beautiful beach.

Sand represents you and your story. Sand represents others and their love for you. Sand represents God's presence in your life — and his promise to be close to you always. It represents his promise to be as close to you as the grains of sand are to each other. May the wish become a reality, and for you may every day be a beach.

Not Just Fly, But Soar

Colossians 3:12-17 – *As God's chosen ones, holy and beloved, clothe yourselves with compassion, kindness, humility, meekness, and patience. Bear with one another and, if anyone has a complaint against another, forgive each other; just as the Lord has forgiven you, so you also must forgive. Above all, clothe yourselves with love, which binds everything together in perfect harmony. And let the peace of Christ rule in your hearts, to which indeed you were called in the one body. And be thankful. Let the word of Christ dwell in you richly; teach and admonish one another in all wisdom; and with gratitude in your hearts sing psalms, hymns, and spiritual songs to God. And whatever you do, in word or deed, do everything in the name of the Lord Jesus, giving thanks to God the Father through him.*

You would expect that two members of the United States Air Force would know what is distinctive about December 17, 1903. You don't have to be in the military to associate that date with the aeronautical event at Kitty Hawk. Some of you may even remember which man held the controls and which man held on to the rope. But we don't all remember which man was which, because history has linked the two and simply calls them The Wright Brothers. Which of them was the more significant? Wilbur tried to fly first but it was Orville who got things off the ground. It was Wilbur who held tight and kept him safe, however. But do you suppose they quarreled about power, responsibility, fame, and blame? Perhaps. Some brides and grooms still do. *It was my idea*, he said. *I did it better*, she replied. *But I was there to stave off disaster*, says he. *Which it would have been if we'd done it your way*, says she.

What then shall we say about these words from the letter to the Colossians: "Clothe yourselves with compassion, kindness, humility, gentleness, and patience. Bear with each other and forgive grievances you may have against each other. Forgive as the Lord forgave you. Over all these virtues put on love, which binds them all together in perfect unity." Most of all, remember that some days the two of you will be Wilbur and Orville individually, and some days you will be the

Wright Brothers together. Both descriptions are accurate and desirable. Although unity is the word in scripture, it doesn't mean some lockstep that takes away your individual personalities. You each were you alone before this day you become you together. Wilbur had his job and Orville had his talents; sometimes they were shared and sometimes they were exchanged. Sometimes shared and exchanged and sometimes challenged and affirmed, in order that their grand experiment would be conducted and we all could fly.

It is not that the concept of flight was new at Kitty Hawk. It wasn't even new with Leonardo da Vinci. Remember the words of the prophet Isaiah who, admitting that not every day is perfect, reminds us that there is a weariness that can consume us. But surely knowing that the Wilburs and Orvilles of this world would never fly as long as they were apart, Isaiah wrote, "Those who hope in the Lord will renew their strength. They will soar on wings like eagles." Oh, and I like the image. That with God, we will fly. And not just fly, but soar. Can move higher than anyone could ever have imagined.

Unless we're talking about your own imagination, that is. Imagining that you could come from your separate spots, separate families, separate histories, and be at a Kitty Hawk of your own, listing your strengths, merging your talents, and sharing your love. Taking the example of those who have flown before you, and make it your own — knowing that not all of the strength, hope, and joy comes from inside you, but from God himself. Knowing that if Kitty Hawk is known as first in flight, then your marriage will be known as first in love.

Wilbur and Orville, The Wright Brothers — it is scriptural, that the two shall become one. It is not worrying whether it is about Richard or Susan, but knowing that Susan and Richard are blessed by God who has called you and promises to fly with you always. Blessed by God who promises to soar with you always, and delights in the trip.

You'll Never Ride Alone

Ecclesiastes 3:1-8 – *For everything there is a season, and a time for every matter under heaven: a time to be born, and a time to die; a time to plant, and a time to pluck up what is planted; a time to kill, and a time to heal; a time to break down, and a time to build up; a time to weep, and a time to laugh; a time to mourn, and a time to dance; a time to throw away stones, and a time to gather stones together; a time to embrace, and a time to refrain from embracing; a time to seek, and a time to lose; a time to keep, and a time to throw away; a time to tear, and a time to sew; a time to keep silence, and a time to speak; a time to love, and a time to hate; a time for war, and a time for peace.*

They say that it's easy to be a winning race car driver. You just go to NASCAR.com and buy a safety helmet or a fancy team jacket, and there you are. They say that it's easy to be married. You just go to the mall to buy a pretty gown and get measured for a tuxedo, and there you are. They say that it's simple to be a good race car driver. You just start it up, do what everybody else does, and stay out of trouble. They say that it's simple to be married. You just start it up, do what everybody else does, and stay out of trouble. They say that it's fun to be a race car driver. People clap for you, take your picture, and give you money. Maybe that's the story of your wedding day too.

It is only because you two and your families like auto racing so much that I use the NASCAR image. But whether we're talking about race car drivers or marriage, it comes to this: if you think it's all about you, you're wrong. For a few hours today, it's hard to argue that it's *not* all about you. You'll find that the personal attention quickly fades and soon enough you'll be on your own. You will be on your own for the event that starts today and continues. It is a ride that's sometimes exciting, sometimes boring, sometimes dangerous, and always hard work. If it goes well, when friends and family look at your marriage and congratulate you on how well you're doing, when they say that you're winners, resist the temptation to take all the credit. Even the most successful race car driver knows it's not all about him. Everyone knows that a pit crew, a sponsor, race officials, and fans like you and me combine to make a winning team what it is. Many people will help make your marriage strong too.

You must have known that, because you chose for the first lesson today a picture that speaks of strength. The passage from Ecclesiastes says that a single cord is strong. But greater strength comes when two cords are wound together. If you want something even stronger than that, try three strands. That's obvious today. Though each of you alone brings strength into any situation you'll face, the two of you together create a strength that is more than double. And the third cord? Well, identifying the third cord and depending on the third cord is what could make all the difference in your marriage. True wisdom is realizing that it's the third cord that keeps you bound together and strong, the cord that makes you a winning team — three cords, bound together... bound.

To be bound with someone you love is good but to be confined in a relationship you hate is bad. To be wrapped up in a task can be good but to be trapped doing something you hate is bad. To be tied together can be good but to be tied up is not. The question before you today is, *In this whole matter of binding, to what do you want to be tied?* You wish to be tied to each other, certainly, and to the Lord too. But do you need to be tied to the past? Probably not. Do you need to be tied to your families? You need that less now than before. Do you need to be tied to your jobs, your hobbies, and your friends? Maybe you do, but there are priorities. You can't be tied deeply to everything, nor should you be. Scripture says, "For this cause of marriage, you leave behind what was and get bound up in what will be." You stop and you start. Like the line in the pavement at the race track, where you both start and stop. That is the way it is with life. Some things begin and others end. Some things wrap and some come loose. There's a time for everything. Wisdom understands what and when that time is. Wisdom understands most of all what it is that makes being bound together tolerable, wonderful, loving, and eternal.

That's the example of Christ, the third cord, who pulls us tightly to himself, who binds us to himself with a pleasant cord, and nothing that strangles. It's a binding that will not let go, no matter how much we might work against it. It is a binding that offers strength and sustenance, something that endures through good and bad, and something that gives without requiring in return. That is what's important in your marriage, isn't it? That you choose to be with each other, bound up with Christ and the rest of the team, his people, the church. You are never alone, you are always accompanied. You are tied with others around you who help you, care about you, who pray for you, and hope for your future. This is the body of Christ, your support team, your sponsor, and pit crew, the people of God throughout history and around the world. Some of them have left you a good example. Some of them invite us to learn from their sadness. All of them rejoice in the three cords that bring strength. Three cords — Carl, Traci, and Christ. Three cords — faith, hope, and love — the past, the present, the future. Three strong cords — God who is Creator, Savior, and Helper. On it goes. Three strands that bind you and all of us together with cords that will not be broken.

They say that it's easy to be a race car driver. It is, if you know that you never ride alone. May you know that in your marriage too — that this day and every day, forever and ever, you never ride alone.

Regifting? Sure It's Okay

Colossians 3:12-17 – *As God's chosen ones, holy and beloved, clothe yourselves with compassion, kindness, humility, meekness, and patience. Bear with one another and, if anyone has a complaint against another, forgive each other; just as the Lord[a] has forgiven you, so you also must forgive. Above all, clothe yourselves with love, which binds everything together in perfect harmony. And let the peace of Christ rule in your hearts, to which indeed you were called in the one body. And be thankful. Let the word of Christ dwell in you richly; teach and admonish one another in all wisdom; and with gratitude in your hearts sing psalms, hymns, and spiritual songs to God. And whatever you do, in word or deed, do everything in the name of the Lord Jesus, giving thanks to God the Father through him.*

Five days before Christmas, five minutes before the moment you've anticipated, it seems right to speak of gifts. You'd think that gift-giving is simple. But almost everyone knows that it's not. That's because gift-giving is full of decisions, hard decisions, heavy decisions, and implication-filled decisions. Right now, the basic question is, who should receive a gift and who should not. Once that is determined, you need to ask if the recipient gets a big gift or a stocking stuffer. If a big gift, is it a gift long remembered or an amount of cash? If it is a gift long remembered, is it something you yourself would appreciate? There is an expectation involved. You think I'm speaking of Christmas — though in fact I'm talking about your life together.

In the next year, and in ten years from now, what is the gift you will give to each other? For Valentine's Day, for your birthday, for any old Tuesday, what will you give each other? Will it be something grand or a peck on the cheek? Will it be something everyone else has or something unique? Will it be something you yourself would like? Are there expectations involved? Oh heavens, more expectations than you will admit. That is part of the problem. We get so involved in our giving and receiving that the whole purpose of it is almost lost, until we read again the scripture you just heard. We heard how it is that God has given each of us a great gift and that he expects it to be given again. In today's world, re-gifting is a bad word. But in God's eyes, it's the way things should be done. That what you receive, you give on — and give again and again. Assuming, that is, that you know what is the gift God has given you, and what good it is. The gift of life, to be sure, is good to re-gift. The gift of love, and the gift of personality, sharing, sacrifice, joy, compassion, hope, and patience. All that you have received is there for you to give.

If it were all that simple, your marriage would be as happy a time as is Christmas. But Christmas isn't always a happy time. Some people say, *I don't like the pressure. I don't like the commercialism. I don't like the choices. I don't like the prices. I don't like the selection. I don't like my relatives. At Christmas, I'll give. But I won't like it.* The problem there is that you think the giving of gifts must begin with you. In truth, scripture tells us that the beginning of gifts lies with God, so that you don't need to be creative; you need to be generous. You don't need to be selective; your list should be long. You don't need to hurry; you should take your time to be sure that you understand what you have received and delight in all the ways you can share it. Each of you — both of you — in this next week, and always, should share it.

I don't know exactly why you chose Christmas to be married. Maybe it was the schedule. Maybe it was the decorations. Maybe it was the romance. But I hope you considered that Christmas is the time of God's perfect gift, given to you and all of us as an example for your own perfect giving to each other. It is giving lots, not a little; forever, not just now. Grace is not a requirement. Five days before Christmas. Five minutes before those words that bind you together as recipients and as givers this day, and forevermore.

More Than A Pile Of Rocks

Matthew 7:24-27 – *"Everyone then who hears these words of mine and acts on them will be like a wise man who built his house on the rock. The rain fell, the floods came, and the winds blew and beat on that house, but it did not fall, because it had been founded on rock. And everyone who hears these words of mine and does not act on them will be like a foolish man who built his house on sand. The rain fell, and the floods came, and the winds blew and beat against that house, and it fell — and great was its fall!"*

Every bride and groom gets gifts. It's one of the ways that society outfits you for life. Every bride and groom gets towels and silverware, china and sheets. Many brides and grooms get prayers. But not every couple gets rocks. You have asked something of us today. You've asked us to gift you with a pile of rocks. Stones you gave us first, but stones we will change before we give them back to you. Stones that will become in your life a kind of cairn.

I was a young boy at summer camp when I first became aware of cairns. Cairns are piles of rocks that people set up. Those piles of rocks were reminders of some place and time that was special. They are piles of rocks that had a promise and a prayer attached. Cultures throughout time have built altars, have made cairns, and have used rock to say about a moment in time — this is unique. What else could I wish for two geologists about to be married? Just this — that your life may be rocky.

Not rocky in the sense that there will be trouble, but rocky in the sense that there will be stability. Rocky in that there will be strength and that there will be a foundation. Though I admit to a bias in my suggestion of foundation. Every marriage is built on something. I suggest that yours be built on the love of God shown through Christ Jesus, a model worthy of your imitation. That as God has loved us first, that we are to love each other. That as God has loved us sacrificially, we are to give over to each other. That as God has forgiven us, we pardon each other. That as God's love is steadfast and immovable, yours will be too.

That's all logical, isn't it? It's what you assume on a day like this. Then why is there so much failure? Perhaps because some couples see digging through rock as hard work and not as a means of discovery. Some people gather up stones to throw instead of rocks to build. Some people try to build when they have nothing that acts as a base. There may be no stones at the beginning but you have asked us to build you a cairn. You asked for a pile of beautiful rocks that will recall not just this day, and not just these guests, but the whole of eternity that is the time and place of God's rich love.

You've asked us to pray on these rocks. Not to make them idols or little gods, but to use them as a focus for what blessings we ask God to give you today. Some will ask that you receive wisdom. Some will pray for your courage. Others will think of delight or patience, wisdom or good humor. My own prayer is that in your marriage you remember what you learned in school, that you have the sense to tell gold from pyrite. Have the sense to tell real gold from fool's gold. I pray that you may know what is authentic and what is not. Then, to be certain that your love is that authentic — as authentic as is the love shown you today. Be certain in knowing that the that best love of all is from God.

Today, that you may have something to remember, we give you a cairn. A pile of rocks. Ordinary stones that become extraordinary because of our love for you. A love we know how to give because it was given to us first. Given to us by the God who made the rocks and you, and blessed it all.

What's In Your Junk Drawer?

1 Corinthians 13 – *If I speak in the tongues of mortals and of angels, but do not have love, I am a noisy gong or a clanging cymbal. And if I have prophetic powers, and understand all mysteries and all knowledge, and if I have all faith, so as to remove mountains, but do not have love, I am nothing. If I give away all my possessions, and if I hand over my body so that I may boast, but do not have love, I gain nothing. Love is patient; love is kind; love is not envious or boastful or arrogant or rude. It does not insist on its own way; it is not irritable or resentful; it does not rejoice in wrongdoing, but rejoices in the truth. It bears all things, believes all things, hopes all things, endures all things. Love never ends. But as for prophecies, they will come to an end; as for tongues, they will cease; as for knowledge, it will come to an end. For we know only in part, and we prophesy only in part; but when the complete comes, the partial will come to an end. When I was a child, I spoke like a child, I thought like a child, I reasoned like a child; when I became an adult, I put an end to childish ways. For now we see in a mirror, dimly, but then we will see face to face. Now I know only in part; then I will know fully, even as I have been fully known. And now faith, hope, and love abide, these three; and the greatest of these is love.*

In the midst of all the happiness of this day, taking note of all the loving greetings sent your way, in front of all your family and friends, this is my advice to you: through all your married life, remember to keep your closets clean. It's the one thing people often ignore. We take such good care of most of what belongs to us. We mop our kitchen floors and wax our cars. Some people organize the china cabinet and the tools in the garage. The bedroom and the bathroom are spotless. But not all of us keep our closets clean, with the result that stuff builds up. And a lot of what fills our closets is junk.

Think about the junk drawer most homes have. What's kept there didn't start out as junk, to be sure. But someone tossed in an old rubber band and someone found a thumb tack. Junk drawers are good for spare batteries and little plastic clothespins. But the pens are dried up and the coupons are out of date. And that's just one drawer. The bedroom closet hides worn out blouses, atrocious ties, and sweaters you never liked. Another closet holds the supplies for hobbies long-forgotten and the equipment for sports no longer played. Still another holds the childhood things your parents now insist belong to you. Doesn't anybody ever get rid of things? Doesn't anybody ever get rid of things they don't like? Doesn't anybody ever get rid of things that aren't any good? Please realize that I've stopped talking about the closets in your house and started talking about the closets in your lives.

The junk that builds up in a marriage didn't start out as junk. Today's scripture lesson said that love is patient and kind. But when the bride starts to remember exactly how patient she was and the groom remembers how many times he was kind, the closet starts to fill up. When the bride and groom keep lists, not of presents received but of opportunities that were missed, and when tears come from pain more than joy, when memories are collected only to seek an advantage, you're well on your way to junk. Some people throw into their closets everything that went wrong and all the expectations of what never went right. Some brides collect resentment and some grooms stack up anger. It's part of our sin that we all store away the ammunition we think we'll need for fights that should never happen. You may not even realize that it's happening. Most people don't. But most people don't start out with junk drawers and filled cabinets. They grow one piece at a time, until it all becomes overpowering. Life that is not love, life that is envious and boastful, love that is arrogant and rude seems to increase in size, and some days it even spills out of the closet.

It would seem right that when the closets grow crowded, we should do some cleaning. But logic doesn't always count, and we do foolish things. When the pain and disappointment of marriage gets too great, some people build larger houses to store all the junk stuffed in their closets. But that's not what Paul meant when he wrote that love bears all things, believes all things, hopes all things (and) endures all things. He never meant that love must collect all things. Unless, of course, what you collect is the greatness of your sacrifice for each other and the greatness of your love for each other. If the closet is too full of junk, where will you find space for what is great and what is good? Clearly, you have to get rid of something. Wisdom means knowing what to keep.

Keep your love. Keep your respect. Keep your laughter. Keep your amazement. Keep your perspective. Keep your memories. In your closet there's room enough for all of that, because that which is good can be kept in life's tiniest places, while that which is evil swells until it kills. But the choice is yours and the advantage too. For if you collect what is loving and love one another as God has loved you, you won't need the great space of a house because you'll have the great room of a home. The peace that passes all understanding will keep your hearts and your minds.

O perfect Love, all human thought transcending,
    lowly we kneel in prayer before thy throne,
    that theirs may be the love which knows no ending,
    whom thou forevermore dost join in one.

O perfect Life, be thou their full assurance,
    of tender charity and steadfast faith,
    of patient hope and quiet, brave endurance,
    with childlike trust that fears nor pain nor death.

Grant them the joy which brightens earthly sorrow;
    grant them the peace which calms all earthly strife,
    and to life's day the glorious unknown morrow
    that dawns upon eternal love and life.

Dorothy Frances Blomfield 1858 – 1932
(in the public domain)

About the Author

The Rev. Dr. John R. Nagle was educated in the public schools of Pennsylvania and received his Bachelor of Arts degree from Gettysburg College, his Master of Divinity degree from the Lutheran Theological Seminary in Gettysburg and his Doctor of Ministry degree from Drew University. He was ordained into the Gospel Ministry on May 25, 1969, and was pastor of Christ the King Lutheran Church in Cary, NC, from 1969 until 2005. In retirement, he has served in a variety of interim posts. He has served on numerous church, community and state-wide boards of directors, and was the author of various devotional materials, and five books of his sermons: *Teddy the Bartender*, *Carp in Your Trout Stream*, *Her Potato Salad Was Loved by All*, *Happy Birthday Jesus*, and *The Story I Love to Tell*.

He is married to Lanie, the former Elaine Ann Hartzell. They are the parents of two children with two grandchildren. Pastor Nagle has a passion for genealogy and has traced over 15 lines of his ancestors to the sixteenth century and earlier.

He and his wife have traveled to over 125 countries on all seven continents.

www.ingramcontent.com/pod-product-compliance
Lightning Source LLC
Chambersburg PA
CBHW032021090426
42741CB00006B/695